Steelhead River Journal

SKEENA

SKEENA

Rob Brown

Frank Amato

PORTLAND

Steelhead River Journal
SKEENA

Volume 3, Number 1

MIKE WHELPLEY

About the Author

Rob Brown was born in Vancouver B.C., in 1949. He is a longtime member, and director, of the Steelhead Society of British Columbia. He is the former chair of the Steelhead Society's Wild Steelhead Campaign. He has written articles for *Field & Stream*, *Fly Rod and Reel*, *B.C. Outdoors*, *Steelhead Fly Fishing Journal*, the *Vancouver Sun*, the *Interior News* and writes a weekly column, "The Skeena Angler" for the *Terrace Standard*.

A teacher for over twenty years, Brown now divides his time between his family, teaching on call, teaching guitar, writing, and playing in an ageing combo called the Low Budget Blues Band.

Dedication

To Myron Kozak who chased light and captured some of its finest facets, on mountain peaks, on floors of valleys and in the eyes of people.

Subscription Information

One year (four issues) $35.00, Two years (eight issues) $65.00. (Foreign orders add $5.00 per year.) Single copy price $15.95. Send check or credit card information to: **Frank Amato Publications, Inc.**, P.O. Box 82112, Portland, Oregon 97282 or call 800-541-9498, Monday through Friday, 9am to 5pm, Pacific Standard Time.

Publisher
Frank W. Amato

Editor
Frank W. Amato

Graphic Production
Kathy Johnson

About the Cover: Chris Reesor fishing a Skeena River tributary. Photo by Myron Kozak

All photographs taken by the author unless otherwise noted.
Myron Kozak photographs on pages 6, 8-9, 32-33
Frontispiece and title page photograph: Myron Kozak
© 1996 by Rob Brown
Printed in Hong Kong
ISBN: 1-57188-032-1   UPC: 0-66066-00223-5

SKEENA RIVER

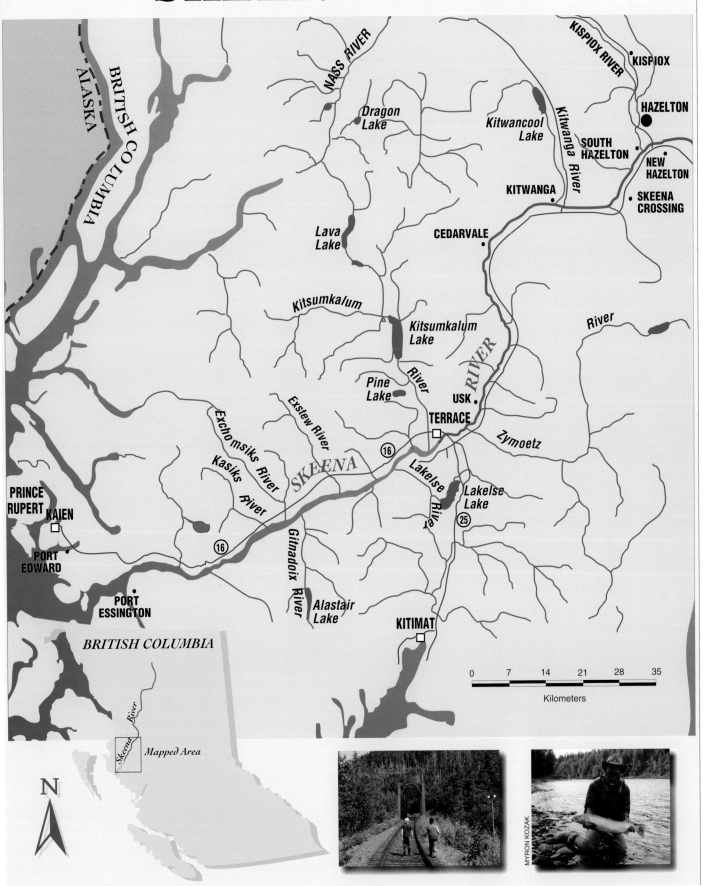

ALASKA

BRITISH COLUMBIA

KISPIOX RIVER

NASS RIVER

Dragon Lake

Kitwancool Lake

Kitwanga River

KISPIOX

HAZELTON

SOUTH HAZELTON

NEW HAZELTON

KITWANGA

SKEENA CROSSING

Lava Lake

CEDARVALE

Kitsumkalum

Kitsumkalum Lake

River

River

Pine Lake

RIVER

River

USK

TERRACE

Zymoetz

Exstew River

Exchomsiks River

Kasiks River

SKEENA

16

Lakelse River

Lakelse Lake

25

PRINCE RUPERT

KAIEN

PORT EDWARD

16

Gitnadoix River

Alastair Lake

KITIMAT

PORT ESSINGTON

BRITISH COLUMBIA

Skeena River

Mapped Area

N

| 0 | 7 | 14 | 21 | 28 | 35 |

Kilometers

MYRON KOZAK

SKEENA

South Town

Clifford introduced me to Skeena steelhead. He was twelve years old, I was twice that. I'd taken a job teaching school in South Hazelton, signing on in mid term to replace a young first year teacher whose nerves had given out. I landed in Smithers and took the bus north through the Bulkley Valley to Hazelton where I was met by the Principal, who assured me the class I was about to assume was not really that bad. "They'd just been allowed to get a little out of control," he said.

He dropped me off in front of a two room teacherage next to the South Hazelton School, in the heart of the small mill driven community the inhabitants of the Hazeltons call South Town. After stowing my luggage—one suit, duffel bag filled with clothes, a guitar and a well worn fly rod—I went out to look around town. The tour didn't take long, there being only a cluster of trailers, a hardware store, a garage, a motel named for a frontiersman named Cataline, and a bar surrounded by logging trucks and 4x4 pickups.

It was a cold March day. Imposing mounds of hard snow still plugged the corners where plows had pushed them. Low cloud cover obscured the distances. I returned to my new home to put things in order and prepare for the next day, my first experience with what turned out to be far and away the most demanding and challenging class of children I was to encounter in my career: one

of those unfortunate groupings of children teachers colloquially refer to as a zoo.

It took one day for me to realize why my predecessor had made a hasty getaway. With a handful of exceptions my charges came from wrecked homes. Most of them, including some of the girls, swore like troopers. Since the majority of my pupils had learned almost nothing in the previous six years of schooling they had plenty of frustrations which they vented by vandalizing the classroom or by pounding on their peers. At first they were impervious to my entreaties but gradually I won them over, building trust and gaining grudging acceptance by devoting almost all my time outside of school to extracurricular activities. For example, every night I opened the gym to my pupils and their older brothers so we could play the most combative variation of round ball I've ever witnessed. Only Clifford remained outside of my control, scowling, uncommunicative and hostile.

Clifford had failed a couple of grades. He was small for his age, so he didn't appear physically out of place in a grade seven class, but he was out of place emotionally. One day I looked up from helping one of the other children apply finishing touches to her puppet to see Cliff leaning across the aisle. "Hey Walter," he said, holding up his bearded, gray-haired puppet in one hand while wielding a pair of scissors in the other, "Mr. Brown." Then he plunged the blades into the skull of the effigy. Another time I saw Clifford looking out the window. He was smiling. I'd never

Lower Skeena at the tidal reach. Mike Whelpley photo.

meal, I grabbed my rod and drove toward a small pond on the edge of town. According to a freckled kid named Darren, whose fishing skills were legend among his classmates, it contained some monster trout. Small fish are big to little people. I suspected the pond, like the others I'd fished recently, would probably be filled with ten inch tarpaper trout, but that was fine.

On the way through town I saw Clifford standing alone, as usual. Impetuously, I stopped the truck and rolled down the window. "Do you like to fish?" I don't know what possessed me. I'd just spent a frustrating day trying to manage Cliff and his classmates, now here I was inviting him into my leisure time. He gave me one those searing looks, hesitated, then said, "Sometimes." He spat the word out.

"Get in." It was an order. To my surprise, I did not receive Cliff's usual profane response, one for which I'd ejected him from class so many times. He calmly climbed in the truck as if he were accepting a dare.

I knew it was useless to attempt small talk. We drove to West's farm. After parking the truck next to a rotting barn I grabbed the fly rod from the front seat, then took the stout spinning rod I'd purchased at the hardware store from the box of the truck. The proprietor said nothing lighter than that rugged piece of glass fiber would do for the salmon that were due to arrive at the junction of the Skeena and Bulkley rivers soon. It was too big for trout, but I didn't think Clifford would care, that is, if I could get him to fish at all.

We walked through the chickens and barking dogs, through the gate and across the spongy approach to the pond. I kept a sidelong eye on Clifford. He seemed unsure of himself on the floating sphagnum, and even more tentative when I ushered him into the leaky old row boat Darren told me would be there. I wasn't that confident myself. There were a pair of planks for oars. I handed one to Cliff. He snatched it from my hand as if it were an unwelcome charity he was forced to accept.

The setting was magnificent: rolling farm on one side, Roche de Boule, the steepest and highest mountain stood sentinel on the other. As we rowed out onto the pond the sound of rock rolling down steep battlements reverberated through the valley. Red winged blackbirds serenaded us. Cliff pointed at the tea coloured water. "Look," he said. There was actually a hint of wonder in voice. A glimmer of expression flickered across his stone countenance. I followed a line from his finger to where wads of frogs were clambering over one another, mating near the reeds. "They look like pickles," he said getting dangerously close to breaking into a smile.

"Watch," I instructed, threading a writhing worm onto a hook then sending it out into the lake below a small weight and a red and white plastic bobber. "When the float goes down..."

"Yeah, I know," said Clifford impatiently.

I scrambled to correct myself, erase any hint of patronage. "Of course you do."

It didn't take long for the bobber to disappear. Cliff struck

seen a smile on his face until then. Quietly I eased over to the windows to find out what had triggered this uncharacteristic response. On the front lawn of the school two of the unkempt and uncared for dogs that prowled the grounds in packs were tearing apart a cat. Cliff was haunted.

School work, not surprisingly, was not high on Clifford's agenda. It wasn't that he couldn't do the work, on the contrary, he was exceptionally bright; he just didn't want to put out the effort, and he wasn't about to be pushed around. He quickly figured out there was little to fear in my puny arsenal of disciplinary techniques. I was paid to see he did it. Cliff and I were at war, and he was winning one battle after another. We were both failing.

Of all the problems in that class, I found Cliff's the most compelling. I suspected Cliff was the product of an abusive home, and I was inexperienced and naive enough to think that things done in school could somehow distract a tortured boy from the dysfunctional family beatings he'd been dealt from his first conscious moments—and quite possibly before that. I tried everything I could think of to motivate him. Nothing worked. Day after day he sat behind the psychic fortress he'd erected and glowered at his classmates, who feared him more than they feared my reproach. He was getting to me. But, he did show up every day, something, I learned from my colleagues, he had not done in earlier grades. Perhaps, I thought, he enjoys the battle, or possibly I've established a connection, sown a seed that may be nurtured.

After my first few days in South Town the clouds lifted revealing the most ruggedly beautiful landscape I'd ever seen. On weekends I explored the rivers and poked around beaver ponds with my fly rod following maps created from what I could glean from my charges as well as people I met in restaurants and the local bar. The days were getting longer. I had four hours of fishing after my school work was finished, a happy occurrence that helped make the daily struggles in class bearable.

One Friday late in the term, after a typically dreadful canned before I was able to tell him to. He winched a little black cut-throat to the boat then derricked it aboard. I whacked its head against the gunwale as Cliff watched intently. Cliff's worms caught six trout before darkness chased us ashore. My flies caught none which, I could tell, pleased him a lot.

When I dropped him off at home, a structure more shack than house surrounded by the rusting corpses of long, low-slung formerly luxurious American cars from a bygone age, I didn't expect him to say thanks. He didn't. "We'll do this again," I said. It was a question and a command. "Yeah," he said, "I know a good place."

He did. I arranged for us to go on a Friday. Cliff showed up with his own rod. After ten minutes, following instructions delivered in his usual laconic manner we arrived at the mouth of a small, steep creek that joined the Bulkley a mile below Hagwilget Canyon. We were at the bottom of a gorge. The shape of the place made you want to look up. As I admired the setting, the steep high cutbanks, the Bulkley surging out of the narrow, dangerous canyon, Clifford started catching fish, good sized Dolly Varden.

The thick brush barred me from the creek proper, but I was able to cast a fly out into the spot where it melded with the Bulkley. This was fortunate for a steelhead snapped up my wet fly and ripped up and down the river with such enthusiasm that even Cliff got excited. It was a tough little fish, yet anyone seeing our revelry from a distance might have presumed we'd beached a world record.

There was no thought of releasing this little beauty, and even if I'd entertained such a notion, there would have been no time to call off Cliff who had been watching the fish like a retriever following the fall of a duck. When the fish slid into the shallows he pounced, rock in hand and killed it with a blow to the brain. To celebrate we found the shade of a cottonwood. I toasted the fish and our luck with a cold beer, Cliff hoisted a coke. We ate sandwiches, rye bread stuffed with pepper salami and cheese, listened to the distant roar of the river, of the tattoo of ruffed grouse, the songs of the first birds of spring, and I decided this was as fine an angling experience as I'd experienced, and pledged to find more of these handsome fish.

The school year was winding down. The class was under control, even Cliff did a little work. As it meant a loss of status in the eyes of his peers, open cooperation from him was out of the question, but the sullen defiance was gone. We fished one more time. By then we were actually conversing. Being a native Cliff had, of course, spent a lot of time at Gitxan fishing sites with his elders. With prompting from me he named a number of these locations, spots I returned to and fished over the years. I hooked another steelhead, and lost it. Cliff spent most his time trying to get close enough to stone a bank beaver, a tasty animal, he assured me.

It was long past dinner when I dropped Cliff at home. It was the last time I saw Cliff. I glanced in the rearview mirror as I drove off. He waved. It was a fleeting gesture, but he did wave.

Kitwanga River: Nekt and D.V. Shaw

At feasts dancers manipulate the cords of disclosing masks. Cedar is set in motion, scripted by history passed on by word of mouth. Shapes change. Raven to man, man to raven, bear to man, man to bear. The past is animated; on the poles that stand in Kispiox and Gitanmax and Kitwancool and in Git Wan Gax it is frozen: frames of Gitxan history captured in cedar by skilled carvers. At its top the pole of Nekt has a replica of the trap door that led to the escape tunnels dug through the mound from which

the warlord, leader of the Gitxan of Git Wan Gax, the man who turned to bear in battle, stood and scanned the landscape.

To the south he saw mountains so tall that clouds were often snagged by their snow covered spires. Between the seven jagged crags blue glaciers rested. To the east the Skeena poured out of the Kispiox Range. To the north the Kitwanga River flowed through a wide fertile valley, past the village of the Gitanyow. To the west, the direction from whence parties of Tsimshan warriors came in search of food, slaves, crests, and power, the great Skeena flowed to the sea. On his right, one arm of the extensive trail network that brought traders bearing boxes filled with the precious eulachon grease climbed an aspen covered hillside. To his left Nekt surveyed the natural highway that provided him and his people with fish year-round. A hundred feet below the mound he watched his people harvest the berries growing profusely on the wide fertile plain. This was a place that kept people healthy and strong and happy. It was worth protecting. Nekt expended much energy to do that.

Below the trap door and Nekt's mother's crest, the thunderbird, the carver has captured Nekt in wood. He wears a ferocious mask calculated to unnerve the most worthy foe. Over slate and wood turned to armour, he has pulled the skin of a grizzly. In his hand he holds the strike-only-once club, the supernaturally charged weapon that killed so many marauders.

The pyramid so generously left by the retreating glaciers was flattened at Nekt's orders to accommodate the stilts upon which five houses transformed from cedar by Git Wan Gax carpenters were set. Battlements of sharpened poles were erected for a perimeter. As an early warning system against marauders seeking to surprise his people under cover of night, Nekt commanded that deer hooves be dried then strung around the stockade and throughout the surrounding lands. This done, the shrewd warlord commanded his workmen to lash heavy logs, the Kanugyet, to the base of the fort with cedar bark turned to rope. Tsimshian raiders, victims of the rolling logs, surprise and agony on their faces, flattened bodies, arms and legs splayed, are chiseled upon Nekt's pole, above Maxkyawl, the whole being Nekt found floating on a log in Kitwancool Lake, and Gepigem, the flying frog who straddled the cosmic zones of water, earth and air.

Led by the terrifying figure of their grizzled general the army of Nekt was an imposing force made more formidable by stories that put cosmic forces in their camp.

In the end the stratagems of Nekt were not enough to prevent his fall. Legend has it that a bullet fired from the first rifle introduced to the Skeena Valley pierced his armour and inflicted the fatal wound. The strike-only-once club fell from his hand. Without its head the body fell. The warriors of Git Wan Gax were routed. The victors basked in the glow of the burning fort.

I drove over the bridge to the north side of the Skeena. It was Sunday, the quietest day in native villages, which are always quiet places to begin with. There was no one on the streets. A few aimless mongrels prowled the roads. I bumped across the railway, climbed the hill and turned into the town of Kitwanga, past the mill, trailers, unkempt yards, the gas station, and the small Anglican church, freshly painted, white, and prominent because of its cleanliness. School Road, Short Road, Mill Road, Yard Road, white wooden signs carrying the unimaginative names of a hastily thrown together lumber town that boomed, went bust, settled into a tenuous economic stability and now lies disheveled, an insult to its majestic surroundings.

I drove along the grease trail, now a paved road, parked and walked down the trail to where archaeologists had been digging

into history at the base of Nekt's mound. I climbed to the site of the fort, and looked around as Nekt had. The rush of the swollen river and the sounds of trains and traffic carried over the farm built upon what was once the village of Nekt's followers. In the distance I could see the out buildings of Morgan's farm. I walked down, careful to avoid the digging sites put out of bounds by the archeologists, then walked around the base of mound where I spotted two natives fishing with spinning gear.

It was a hot day, more summer than spring. The two portly men wore runners, jeans and T-shirts. Evidence of bait, jars and wrappers, lay strewn about them. One fisher reeled in to check his hook, cast then lit a smoke. An empty package of Players swirled round and round in a back eddy. "Doing any good?" I called to them. They looked up, a bit surprised.

"Some trout," said the man nearest me.

"Dolly Varden?"

"Yeah, Dollies," answered the man closest to me.

So, here, I thought, was perhaps the direct descendant of Nekt's sergeant at arms or, quite possibly, a direct descendant of the great warlord himself.

A lot had changed in a few hundred years.

The banks and the bottom river reminded me of the Kispiox, as did the aspen covered hillsides overlooking it; though, it was smaller. The first pool was filled with the gray slate from which Nekt's armour was fashioned. This stone and the dark cobble of the bottom darkened the already dark tea coloured water. I hastily swam a Muddler through the run, without result, then walked back to the car and drove upstream looking from the canyon that Rick Shaw told me offered the best and most consistent fishing on the river.

Rick was the first man to hold a guiding license on the lower Skeena River, steering affluent Americans and Japanese to the monster Chinook that seek out the rivers below Terrace. The city had less than a thousand people then and already had an international reputation for excellent angling. But, before he settled there, Shaw spent a few years as principal of the school in Kitwanga. It was a good place for a skillful young man who had honed his angling skills and developed a passion for the sport on the Thompson and Vedder rivers and as a guide in Campbell River.

Most of the good fishing was done in the big pool in the Skeena below its confluence with the Kitwanga. Below that lay an island where trophy steelhead bound for Kispiox and Babine tested the skills of men fishing Cherry Bobbers and balsa spinners. According to Shaw, few anglers bothered fishing the little Kitwanga River at that time, which surprised him when he saw how many fish the natives were able to herd into nets they had fastened to stakes in the river.

When half of the pupils deserted his classes each Easter to follow their parents to the canneries at Prince Rupert, Shaw disregarded the Provincial School Calendar and closed the school. It was during these extended spring breaks that he found steelhead—summer and spring run fish—in the Bard's Hole and the canyon, and at Kitwancool.

Sport fishing the river at the last named place was something of an achievement. Kitwancool is the home the Gitanyow, an isolated village accessible by a rough dirt road. The Gitanyow were not known for their hospitality to the Gumshwa, the white men. There was a report of a forester returning to an overturned pick-up in flames; another of a conservation officer who had been shot in the leg while patrolling near Kitwancool. Thanks to good relations with the parents of his native charges, Shaw had earned some respect and a visa to Kitwancool where the fishing was good and the moose hunting superb. "If I hadn't been forced to transfer because of the job situation, I'd've stayed there forever," he told me.

Aside from the new school and the paved road leading to the village, I suspect Kitwancool is little changed from the time when Rick fished the river running through it. A few children were playing on the river bank, but other than that the place was as tranquil as Kitwanga had been. Few natives have any use for gardens or lawns, quite naturally, since it's not easy to shed thousands of years of hunting and gathering. As a consequence, the air is mercifully free of the whine and whir of lawnmowers, weed whackers and suchlike.

I admired the poles at the centre of town: weather-worn cedar totems crawling with frogs, fireweed, raven, men and bears. After examining some poles lying on the ground that were clearly being restored, and others that were under construction, I walked a few hundred yards and examined the river. It was smaller, no more than a fair sized creek, really. There were places large enough to hide large fish. I was sure some were hiding there. For the most part, natives don't think much of sport fishing and think even less of releasing fish. I added this most recent glimpse of the Kitwanga River to those I'd gathered when Mike Whelpley and I had driven to the outflow at Kitwancool Lake one cold snowy winter, and those I recalled from hikes upstream from the Skeena and downstream from the town to form an impressionistic, incomplete portrait of the river.

Here was a typical summer steelhead river, lake headed with a canyon and enough deep pools to provide comfort and a measure of security for over wintering summer fish. Much of its upper reaches are too bog-filled and brush-lined for ease of access or casting, but at least half the river has decent trails and plenty of room. I suspect the holding water in the latter is very limited making the timing of a fishing trip critical.

Natives, who have always viewed steelhead as a staple since it was the only fresh fish available during the long cold winters, net the river, as they have done for millennia. The salmon, though, are still the most heavily fished species—even more heavily netted since the natives have begun a selective commercial fishery. This activity targets sockeye, however, and most of it is conducted in the Skeena. If anything, this restructured fishery is probably good news for steelhead fishers.

There won't be many summer steelhead in the river of the Gitanyow and the river of the descendants of Nekt, but there probably never was. For a seasoned angler a few fish is plenty. Besides, these are cousins of the Kispiox steelhead, eking out a living at the same northerly latitudes. There will be some large fish like the handsome brutes caught by Rick Shaw, Chuck Ewart and Finlay Ferguson. I've yet to find one, but I'm confident I will.

Finlay Ferguson: A Day at Shames

It's a beautiful place in all seasons, but especially so in summer. We get there by crossing the railway bridge built, according to the date chiseled into its footing, on the eve of the Great War, then walking the path that follows the Shames River. Between the ties we see the river is tinted blue with glacial flour. The first pink salmon of the year have reached the pool under the span. We move downstream. I'm slowed by the raft, which must be dragged over the shallower riffles, Finlay, who was a year old when the bridge was completed, is slowed by age.

We pass ponds filled with salmon fry trapped until fall rains bring the river back to them. Gulls and ravens have left tracks in the gray mud; tracks of moose and bear describe their passage from the woods to the water's edge, up the river, and back into the brush.

Wild meadow flowers grow at the heart of the island that lies between the small and big rivers. Their scent blends with the sharp aroma of cottonwood. A spicy redolence swirls through trembling aspen leaves. The wind is warm.

Fin rests on his staff. I stop as he gazes through the heat haze at the towering cottonwood stand behind the Shames Slough.

"Used to be mostly spruce through here, big ones. Same thing all along the lower river, big stands of spruce. I've seen them come into Sande's Mill, three on a truck. "

"How did they get the trees across the river?"

"Boomed 'em up and took 'em across just below Gallagher's cabin."

"Gallagher?"

"Yeah. Just below where the German fishing lodge is now. Gallagher had a shack right there. He was one of those circus fighters—those guys you'd pay to step in the ring with. If you lasted a round you'd win a hundred bucks. After that he worked for the lumber company. We used to have some poker games in that cabin." Fin's smile is distant.

"One time, after we'd all had a lot to drink, I took exception to something this French Canadian guy said. Dusted him off pretty good. I figured he was down and out. Well, I sit down again and the sonofabitch comes up behind me and breaks a ketchup bottle over my head."

I wince at the thought of it.

"What a mess. They took me to the Emergency Room at Mills Memorial. I came in all covered with ketchup and blood. Should've seen the look on the nurse's face. She thought it was all blood."

"And Gallagher, what happened to him?"

Finlay starts walking, "Killed a guy over a bottle. Blew his head off with a shotgun. They put him away for murder. Gave him a long sentence. He's probably dead now."

Finlay has his breath back. Years of hard rock mining damaged one of his lungs. If it's humid when we make this walk he is forced to stop two or three times and wait for his lung to stop burning. He never complains, but I know he hates these respites. We carry on.

I take the boat up a side channel. Fin takes the shorter route, through the tall grasses where the moose bed down, past the sprawling log jam. We meet at the top the bar.

The river is wide. Rugged mountains, punctuated with glaciers are the backdrop. Alder-lined avalanche chutes sweep down to where black cottonwoods crowd the river banks.

The fish are everywhere. Juvenile salmon, seeking security from marauding char and cutthroat trout, plug the interstices along the rocky beach. Further out in the flow schools of pinks and sockeye push their way upstream. Further out still, giant Chinook roll majestically. Steelhead bound for Kispiox, Babine, Bulkley, Sustut and many lesser-known streams are invisible, but we know they are out there, slipping through the schools of salmon.

With the fish come other predators: the dark heads of seals pop up momentarily then disappear; eagles ride thermals; bears prowl distant banks. We're predators too, Fin and I, not particularly good ones, but good enough to find decent sport.

We start where the Skeena breaks over a shallow, broad riffle, bends around a log jam, then spreads out to glide over a wide shelf. Fish seek these shelves for short periods of rest and relief

Skeena sunset over the lower river. Mike Whelpley photo.

from the heavier main current of the river. The best fishing in the mainstem Skeena is found in these situations. I respectfully call this one Ferguson's Reach for Finlay who, for years, fished it and many other parts of the Skeena with a fly rod while other anglers soaked bait or tossed spoons to salmon. Finlay is an original, a pioneer. When he started exploring the water near home only two other fly fishers fished that method exclusively, but they limited their excursions to the Skeena's lower tributaries, and used only sinking lines.

"Remember the Dutch men and their shooting heads?" I ask Fin who is knotting a fly to his tippet. The upstream view from where we are standing is captured in a picture sent to me by Patrick Mersey, a young Dutch english teacher, who along with his countryman Henk Melse found his way to Ferguson's Reach with the help of a map drawn by me. Seeing that view again triggered the memory.

When the Netherlanders found the river they bumped into Finlay, who gave them some helpful advice, then sat down in the shade of the log jam to watch them catch pink salmon after pink salmon with strange looking flies on the end of short leaders and shooting heads.

Finlay left. The Dutch men stayed on, camping overnight and fishing the next day. On the second day the novelty of catching pink salmon had worn off. Fortunately a trio of steelhead broke the monotony. The image of one is captured on that photograph sent me by Patrick, who can barely get his hand around its tail for the shot. It's one of the largest steelhead I've seen, alive or in pictures, over thirty pounds certainly. On the back of the photo Patrick has written "Twenty pound steelhead released—Skeena River."

"Those fellows could cast an inch less than a mile," says Fin. "I started with those heavy, lead lines, but it was work. They stuck to the bottom. If I had to fish those things every day, I'd quit fishing."

A long time ago Fin concluded that fly fishing was most enjoyable when done with grace and precision. An art not a science, the sport had to be a beautiful thing, a stimulus and counterpoint to analysis and contemplation. After a short stint with leaden lines, he filled his Hardy Zenith with a floater and has fished that way to this day.

I watch him work down the riffle, sending out a long line with his ten-foot six-weight rod. I have watched him hook every kind of fish with this outfit—even an occasional spring salmon.

Finlay likes to catch cutthroat. He also likes Dolly Varden, especially the large ones that find their way to the Skeena riffles late in the year. Salmon are a nuisance to him, steelhead a dividend.

Today we both hook a humpback. Convinced we have devoted enough time to the riffle, we climb in the raft and push off. The boat scrapes against the bottom sending a stone rattling downstream.

We pass Gallagher's point.

"Yes sir, he was a bad bugger."

"Who?"

"Gallagher," replies Fin, apparently amazed that I could have lost the thread of the conversation we'd begun half an hour earlier.

"He'd have a big pot of stew on this old wood stove..."

"Gallagher?"

"Yeah, Gallagher," Fin says with a hint of irritation. "...in this big iron pot. One morning I was there and he'd just got up. The top of the stew was all covered in green mold. Old Gallagher walks up, scoops up a big spoonful, downs it in one gulp and chases it with a half a bottle of stale beer." The image chases thoughts of lunch from my mind.

Riverborne sand hisses under the raft. At the next bend we startle two moose. They're off instantly, the rattle and splash of their hooves in the shallows echoes across the river until they scramble up the bank and disappear into the alder. A copse of red osier and willow, cropped as evenly as a hedgerow along an English country lane, marks the place where they browsed.

Finlay reaches into the green rain jacket given him by Sam the oil man from Wyoming. He pulls out a peppermint tin, opens it with a pop, and plucks a fly and shakes it to disengage it from the tangled mat of nearly identical patterns. It's a Skinny Skunk, a thin concoction dressed on a number eight up eyed hook. The body of this one is a single strand of wool wound tightly. The rib is fine wire. It sports a black beard and a tail of red cock hackle. A few strands of polar bear hair make up the wing.

"What were you using upstream?" I ask.

"Partridge and Orange in a size twelve." Soft hackled flies, this size or smaller, are the mainstay of Finlay's arsenal. I've watched him hook and land some very large steelhead on them.

"We used to fish one pattern, Ted Rawlins and I. Polar and Red. Then I read an article in an American outdoor magazine. It was all about dark flies and how good they were for steelhead. I tried some out and caught more trout with them than I ever had with the old Polar and Red. Had to tie them skinny, though—to get under the water quickly. Started using level leaders, 10 feet of 10-pound test, because they sink quicker."

The next run is large, even in the low, slow waters of spring. Now, in summer flow, it's immense. Our task is to find the smaller river in the larger one. We fish the edge. It's my turn to go first. I choose a sinking line then wade to my waist. The water laps at the ankles of Fin's hip boots. I find a pair of trout. Fin finds a brilliant summer steelhead I missed. The fish uses much of the river. Fin stands his ground and, after 10, maybe 15 minutes, he subdues it.

"Those steelhead move up the river along the edges," Fin says in a matter-of-fact way, as the steelhead hovers in the shallows for a moment then glides out of sight. "You don't need to be too far out to get them."

At Either Island there is one Dolly Varden; at the Radio Run there is nobody home.

Fin says, "The Skeena's like that. One day you think you got it all solved, the next day you get skunked. Did I ever tell you about the time in late November when I found a big school of sea-run cutthroat?"

I say no so I can again enjoy the account of a splendid day's fishing that stands out in the long career of an angler who has had so many fine days.

The rods rest as we spend the next two hours floating—two men in a dinghy, dwarfed by tall mountains and a wide river. We take out where the Germans like to, then drive Finlay's Ford inland along Highway 16 to my rusting Datsun pickup.

It's 10 o'clock when we return to the Shames Bridge. The light is soft. The mountains glow. Fin looks up the Shames Valley. The flood channel is wide and filled with stumps. The river is braided and unsettled.

"That train bridge has stood up since 1914," Fin says. "Look at it now."

Gravel has built up to within a foot of the span.

"One more flood and she'll be gone—unless they dredge the channel."

Fin has watched the river change, slowly at first, then quickly as the pace of logging has accelerated and torrents of debris began rumbling down the valley. Helicopters are lifting the last stands of old timber from the Shames. The bottom of the river and its banks have been set in motion. The river has been uprooted, lost its stability.

"This is happening all over Skeena," growls Fin. "It'll ruin the fishing." He nods his head in the direction of the Shames. "This is where the fishery begins."

As usual, Finlay hits the nail squarely. Almost every watercourse in this valley is reeling from blows dealt it by loggers. Chimdemash, Big and Little Oliver, Legate, Kleanza, all lie on the downstream approach to Terrace along Highway 16. All of them run through steep-sided valleys; all have had vast sections of foliage shorn from their upper watersheds, and all have had their lower reaches ripped apart by devastating floods born of what the meteorologists call rain-on-snow events.

We agree to try the river again in two days. It's 11 p.m. Finlay leaves first. I watch his tail lights vanish. I drive up the hill past Amesbury, over the Zymacord Bridge, and past the small settlement at New Remo. Everything is losing definition in the failing light; larger objects are beginning to loom. Late in the summer evenings of Skeena everything gets darker, but it never really gets dark.

Gene Llewellyn: Keeper of the Copper and Clore

The Copper River is the largest and saddest example of what happens when floods hit a valley given over to industry. Not comfortable with the Tsimshan name Zymoetz, the exploitation-minded white settlers renamed the river for its mineral deposits and for the metallic sheen it assumed after very heavy rain or during periods of runoff—but it wasn't that colour that often, or for that long, according to Gene Llewellyn.

If the Skeena is Finlay's river, the Copper is Gene's. A Terrace native, Gene grew up in the midst of a large family packed into a small cabin a stone's throw from the banks of the Kitsumkalum River.

"The old man used to forget our names. As soon as we were old enough to work, he kicked us out," Gene recalls.

Seventy years later he lives in a small trailer, next to Dutchy and Jim Snodgrass, the landlord who charges no rent, a mile from his beloved Copper River.

Inspired by the oratory of Dr. Norman Bethune, Gene signed on with the Republicans to fight in the Spanish Civil War until a bullet in the hip sent him home. After mending, he swapped dodging bullets for dodging logs. Terrace was a boom town, forests were still felled without towers and grapple yarders, logs were boomed and driven down the Kalum River, new roads opened old valleys. Loggers worked long, hard dangerous hours, collected fat cheques, and, like Gene, often lived fast lives well lubricated with liquor.

"It got so bad I'd open my eyes in the morning and my hands would be shaking so hard I couldn't pour a drink. I'd knock the bottle over onto a plate and lap the booze up like a dog." He shakes his head from side to side then says, "Bad stuff. Like swallowing hack saw blades. Dr. Lee told me if I had one more blackout I'd die. That was almost thirty years ago. I quit smoking and drinking. Haven't done either one since then."

Gene is small, wiry. His skin, the colour of a worn ax handle, is pulled taut over his bony frame. Both his wrists carry wide copper bands to ward off arthritis. We sit at his kitchen table in front of two steaming cups of instant coffee. On the wall behind us hangs a framed couple—beaming bride and serious groom—and a photo of Khutzeymateen grizzlies mating.

"My wedding pictures," he says. His eyes, alert and quick, sparkle from under the peak of the Baltimore Orioles baseball cap.

I ask Gene to tell me about the river he patrols daily from April through January of each year.

"There were pools, runs, real beauties. They didn't open up the valley until 1960. Before that we fished the lower end, to Eleven Mile at the canyon. The fishing was good. We took lots of fish. Some of them were real big. Blackie McConnell took a 28-pound buck from the pool above Baxter's one November."

I ask for more detail.

"There was good water everywhere. Once the road was through to the Fossil Beds, nobody bothered much with the water below the Clore. We just drove up to the Rum Hole and fished down, through One Only, the Bread and Butter, the Fossil Pool, the Bluff, Rawlins', the Road Run, and all them other pools. By that time it'd be dark and our arms would be sore from playing steelhead."

His voice rises for emphasis. "The water was good, blue and clean. It had to rain real heavy before it went out—real heavy. And, then the river cleared real fast."

As Gene paints a vanished landscape, I picture the few remaining pools of the type he describes: splendid pieces of architecture built of ledge rock seams and boulder-filled tail outs.

"There are too many roads too close to the river, too many clear cuts. The pipe line and the transmission towers didn't help...too many floods."

The rivers in Skeena have always known floods. The annual high water in late April, when the main river swelled with snow melt was dramatic, gradual and expected: an occurrence as natural as the greening of the leaves and the lengthening of the days. For the farmers living in the low lands at Old Remo and the residents at Lakelse Lake, these floods were uncomfortable, but far from devastating.

There were years when an unusually heavy snow pack caused serious damage. This kind of inundation was infrequent: fifty year floods when the people of the Skeena Valley braced themselves as the waters of the river swelled over a period of weeks eventually spilling over banks then dikes.

In recent years the fifty-year floods became five-year floods then, for a time, biannual floods, ferocious angry events that came quickly and unexpectedly. Overnight quiet glides swelled and began to hiss. Chattering riffles turned into roaring rapids. Small cascades became waterfalls. The havoc started late in the year with rainfall high in the mountain flanks. Rain falling on snow, an event hitherto almost unknown, became familiar with the onset of globally-warmed winters.

Just when they were settling into the smaller, ice-bound confines of winter, the small mountain creeks, filled up with runoff and began acting as if it was spring freshet. As they grew the little tributaries tore away at their banks, their bottoms were set in motion. Rocks were sent hurtling downstream together with logs, root wads and other debris.

The creeks smashed into roads. The metal culverts plugged up. Road sections exploded. Roadways became creeks then rivers.

The mainstem rivers mirrored and magnified what is going on in the tributaries. Boulders the size of compact cars were yanked from the stream bed and hurled downstream as if they were weightless. Large chunks of the river bank sheared off, cottonwoods, old spruce and alder lost their grips then crashed into the torrent.

By far the worst of these floods took place in the fall of 1978. The first winter snows were working down the mountain sides. The temperature was dropping. The nights were getting clearer and colder. The goats were clearly visible as they grazed the last greenery of the fall on the lower slopes. After many winters in the bush, Skip Warner like all veteran trappers, had a highly developed sense of season. Skip had promised his wife he'd be home early.

The rain began, softly at first. The trapper was surprised, a little uncomfortable. At this high elevation this was unnatural. The following day the clouds closed, swallowed up the narrow valley of the upper Copper, and it began to pour. Hard rain fell all day, all night, then harder rain followed the next day. Warner hopped in his pickup and struck out for home. Creeks were swirling through the sodden forest. Skip started thinking about the possibility of washouts, about being over fifty miles into the wilderness.

The engine of the old pickup fired on the first turn of the key. Warner rattled down Copper Main, splashing through deep puddles and the newly formed creeks running over the road. After traveling only a few miles the trapper got his pickup hopelessly

Gene Llewellyn fishing. Mike Whelpley photo.

stuck in one of them. Grabbing his gun, a can of beans and some matches he set out to complete the journey on foot. The bridge spanning the Clore River at the base of Clore Canyon is 60 feet from the river in normal flows. When the trapper reached it, the river was running over the decking.

As he waded down the road the roar of the Copper and sound of the rain was deafening. He was inured to cold weather, but this wet cold was almost unendurable. He tried to keep his mind off it, but it nagged him—soaked through his skin, neared the core of his being.

The whole valley was coming apart. An ordinary man would have succumbed, but Skip Warner had spent most of his life acquiring the courage and self reliance a trapper needs, the rigours working a trap line demands. He drew on those resources. The steely, focused calm that sets in at times of peril swept over him. Even the rioting river receded into the distance. He thought only of his feet, of moving forward, of surviving. When he reached the lower canyon, by far the biggest in the river, the entire structure was vibrating. The trip took him two days. He arrived in town cold and shivery, and apologized to his wife.

Floods—none of them as devastating as the one that claimed Gordon Doll's cabin and the 100-foot bank upon which it stood and very nearly claimed Skip Warner—but unusually powerful, nonetheless—continued through the eighties. Just when the river started to gain some stability and sculpt some new holding water, unseasonably warm temperatures would chase the freezing line up the mountains and the river would burst its banks yet again. It was a bad decade for fish and fishermen—a time of loss.

My career on the Zymoetz and Gene's overlap for 15 years, but Gene's loss is greater. Here, from the primordial expanses of the Telkwa Pass through two hissing, roaring canyons to the broad, demanding reaches of the lower river, was steelhead water as good as any on earth. This was a river where multiple fish days

were the rule, spectacular catches of large summer-runs not uncommon, and most of the river—as I was first to discover in the late seventies and early eighties—was perfectly suited to the floating line.

The window of opportunity is all but closed now. A light rain will fill the river with silt, and it will stay turbid for long periods.

"In the summer the Skeena was gray and the Copper was blue. Then we lost the summer months, but the river was always blue in September. Then we lost that, but she cleaned up and stayed as clear as gin all winter. Now, you can't even depend on that," Gene says sadly.

Despite the fickle conditions, formerly guided non-residents are no longer alien. They return to the river in increasing numbers driving rental vehicles, taking advantage of the easy access to compete with the guided anglers, may of whom will probably return without guides too.

The forest cover of the Zymoetz continues to be mined; the fifty year floods are now two or three year floods, while lesser torrents are annual. The river will not heal in Gene's lifetime, but he takes comfort in memories.

"We traded some equipment for a helicopter ride, one time," he says, basking in the recollection. "The pilot put us high up in the system, maybe forty miles. We walked out, me an Elmer. Every pool we fished had fish. We caught so many on the first day, we had to lay down and rest in the afternoon. It was like that every day until we reached the road."

There is no need for helicopter now; today Gene's Shangri-la has roads to it. Development pushes into the wilderness, forests fall more quickly than ever, adjustments are made to the pipeline, and the advocates of growth, operating on the absurd assumption that reducing the time it takes to get from Terrace to Telkwa is progress, push for the construction of a highway up the Valley of the Copper and along Limonite Creek.

Good fishing days are infrequent, but Gene's gray Bronco can be seen on the Copper River Road daily. Fueled by reminiscences of fine days and assisted by the expertise honed over many years of angling, the Keeper of the Copper and Clore, as he is known to the local angling fraternity, finds enough steelhead to make the trips worthwhile.

Prospecting on the Clore

The Clore River was named for a black prospector from West Virginia called Arthur Clore. Nadine Asante's History of Terrace reports that anyone who teamed up with Clore felt "he was the best partner a prospector could hope to have." Clore was something of a mystery, never marrying, never speaking of his

Jim Culp releasing a Skeena River Chinook.

American past, referring to Canada as "the land of hope."

For some time the river named after the black prospector was a mystery too. Gene Llewellyn fished it with lures late in the fall when cooler temperatures halted the glacial runoff enabling the river to drop and clear. Only a few parts of the river were accessible, and only a few of them held fish. Gene fished them, often stopping at the trap cabin of his long time friend Gordon Doll before making the drive home. Moose hunters sometimes stopped to wet a line in one of the Clore's pools, but other than that incidental pressure most of the river remained untouched until Jim Culp began exploring it in earnest.

Jim Culp, his wife Shirley and their young family moved to Terrace from Vancouver in 1974, six years after Arthur Clore was laid to rest. He had been a founding member the Steelhead Society of B.C., later served as the organization's president and has remained a director ever since. Jim's name can be found attached to every fish related environmental issue in Skeena for the last two decades. Among other things, he was the sole voice for sportsmen on Department of Fisheries and Oceans advisory committees dominated by commercial fishing interests; he was the sport fishing Ombudsman for the North Coast for a number of years; he was the founder of the Skeena Watershed Sport fisherman's Coalition. When people applaud the innovative initiatives happening in the Skeena, like selective, in-river fisheries, representative committees at all levels, pilot fisheries for sockeye and pink salmon and so on, they are, probably unknowingly, showing their appreciation for something Jim Culp started or had a large hand in shaping.

When he wasn't attending meetings or running his tackle store, or being a dad, Jim fished the rivers near Terrace, especially the Copper and its small sister stream, the Clore. Jim grew up near the banks of the Coquitlam where he learned his steelheading skills. Already an expert gear fisherman when he came to the Skeena Valley he took up the fly after he'd been here a few years. Some of his earliest and fondest experiences fishing that way happened on the Clore, which was then a perfect river to start steelheading with a fly rod. In fact, Jim who gave Pete's Elbow, the Wasp Run and Rob's Run their names, was probably the first angler to fish the fly on the River.

Part of the Clore, the Clore proper, begins life in the ice fields surrounding Corona Peak, the other part begins in the Burnie lakes where the Burnie River gets its start. The two rivers meet at the base of a steep, but by no means impassable canyon, then flow east between rugged crags like Mount Henderson and Pillar Peak for some fifteen miles before joining the Zymoetz, or Copper River.

The river is the Zymoetz in miniature, with rocky glides and boulder studded pools. The landscape is Jurassic: a place of great movements, where fossils record great upheavals. The fish of this primeval are almost indistinguishable from the small fish of the upper Morice, which is understandable since both rivers drain the same country. Like Morice fish, Clore steelhead seem very susceptible to flies fished on top of the water.

I recall vividly, a day when Gil Cobb and I fished the Clore. It was in the last week of November. The leaves were off the trees, the dun coloured sky was close. We fished as close to the bottom as we could. Neither of us caught a fish. As we approached it, I told Gil of the run Jim named for me. I told him how I'd fished it perhaps two dozen times and how it had always given up at least one fish. We arrived at my run and found it intact: fifty yards of classic steelhead run, full of medium sized boulders, running at just the right speed. We ran our flies through it again and again and yet again. Nothing.

I looked apologetically at Gil, then at the leaden sky. The air was colder. Big lazy snow flakes were drifting down into the river. It was getting dark. I convinced Gil to wait so that I might make one more pass. My hands hurt as I changed reels and ran the floating line through the guides. I tied on a bushy termite, waded into the cold up to my knees, and skated the fly through the tail out. After two drifts a fish boiled; after two more he smashed the fly and I had him—a small Clore buck with a prominent red stripe.

A year later my run finally failed me, although I can't really say that, I suppose, since only a small part of it was left after the heavy flood of the previous fall—a brutal affair that turned most of the river inside out and opened a nasty clay seam that fills most of the Clore and much of the Copper with suspended solids.

Mike Whelpley's Wilderness

Gitnadoix, Khasiks, Khyex, Exchamsiks, Exstall, Zymacord, Extew, the larger rivers that feed the broad expanses of the lower Skeena, ran through the dreams of Ferguson and Llewellyn, but since the rivers close to Terrace were lightly fished, and still offered angling as good as a fisherman could wish for, there was no need to range further afield. Until a very few years ago only the intrepid men who struggled through difficult water in long, wooden, prop-driven boats knew what these streams had to offer.

Today jet-legged, aluminum boats have made the trips to them less arduous, but the demands on a river boater's expertise are still great, and the dangers—because the skippers of aluminum sleds range even deeper into the wilderness—still underpin the excursions.

Mike Whelpley has explored more of the fishing frontier than any other Skeena river runner and angler. His prowess with rod and boat are legend, his life the envy of avid outdoorsmen.

"You know Mike Whelpley?" asked Russell Ross. "Man, I seen him on the Kitlope. He comes flying down the river, sees a log, but instead of slowing down, he gives her bananas—jumps clean over that log then turns 360 degrees so he's facing upstream. Then runs up a side channel."

A Haisla log salvager, carpenter and commercial fisherman, Russell is no stranger to boats. The kind of awe he expresses when describing Mike's skills is shared by those who have worked or fished with the stocky, 47-year-old steelheader who, can occasionally be found at his home on River Road when he's not using rivers as roads to new angling opportunities.

A faller working a distant coastal camp told me of a time he was returning to port. "There we were, 80 miles or more from Kitimat. It's wet and cold and there's a good chop. Who comes running out some lonely river but Mike Whelpley—all by himself."

"I was sitting behind a desk in the Bank of Montreal," says Mike. "And, I realized that in thirty years I wouldn't be physical-ly able to do what I wanted to do."

In mid-career, Mike tendered his resignation, kissed off any thought of long-term benefits and security, bought a Zodiac and set off—alone in most cases—to explore the unknown territories of the North Coast.

The inflatable took him to some tight, intriguing corners, but his aspirations required a bigger boat. To this end Mike designed an aluminum craft capable of cutting through the expanses of salt water standing between him and many appetizing coastal streams. He christened the craft Mileed, the Tsimshan name for steelhead, and with money earned working as a fisheries technician serving far-flung native villages to pay for gas and groceries, he set out through mists and tides to realize his dream.

"I have trouble telling where my job ends and my hobby begins," he says happily.

I've spent many hours traveling and fishing with Mike. A trip to the Gitnadoix on April Fool's Day, 1984, is one of many spectacular memories.

Mike had made his first two forays into the watershed in the previous week and was spilling over with enthusiasm. The day was crisp, clear, and free of bugs. The hardwoods were still bare. A few patches of green clung to the base of the slide chutes. The wind bit our faces and hands as we shot across the Skeena. Mike was sheltered behind the console. I was huddled in my oilskin raincoat.

Part of the Clore River Valley in fall colours.

19

*Mike Whelpley watching clouds scroll across a mountainside
in the Valley of the Kasiks.*

━━━━◆━━━━

In March and April the spring floods are still high up the slopes. It's a time of drought. The rivers are close to the gravel, low, like the snow line, clear and cold like the air, difficult to navigate. Twice in the first few miles I jumped from the boat and walked upstream so Mike could negotiate a skinny riffle. On a tight bend before the first slide chute we miscalculated: I stayed aboard, at the price of a shear pin.

"Go fishing," ordered Mike as he brought the boat to the beach. As he rummaged through his tools and found a spare pin, I did. Deep in the wilderness with no contact and little likelihood of company, a small mistake can push you over the edge of comfort into despair: the failure of a small but significant part transforms an engine into an anchor. Mike is keenly aware of the thin line between safety and peril.

In minutes we were off again, threading our way through the large rocks at the bottom of the canyon. The lower floors of the Gitnadoix are steep, fast, and full of obstacles. Mike beached the sled again then took out a chain saw in order to buck off the tip of the newly-fallen spruce that kept us from the rest of the river.

The whine of the saw shattered the short-lived stillness of the valley. I glassed the bottom of another slide and found a herd of goats eating the first greens of the year. Soon the spruce gate was gone. The sound of the jet replaced the sound of the saw. We moved quickly to a wide, flat spot in the river, an appealing run

deep enough and fast enough to give fish comfort.

"Here," Mike said. "Try a surface fly." Clearly this exercise was part of a plan.

I put up my version of one of Harry Lemire's Greased Liners and skated it over the tail of the run, doubting that a late winter fish would climb through icy water after a fly. After a few casts a fish boiled below the lure. After a few more tries the fish took hold then fought doggedly. It was a fine female, maybe 12 pounds, a surprise fish, quite possibly the first steelhead to be taken that way on this river. Mike smiled like a scientist who had just proved a questionable theory to a panel of skeptical peers.

The morning mists climbed the mountains. We fished with determination and success. The earth warmed up. Cornices cracked then broke free kick starting avalanches. By noon the valley had opened its eyes.

Mike pointed out places where hurricane force winds created by the momentum of large slides had torn the tops from trees. Occasionally a giant avalanche will leap across the valley leaving a barrier in its wake. On the highest banks deposits of debris marked the height of the flood waters that followed the collapse of one of those dams of rock, snow, ice and trees.

Between sips of coffee we speculated on the fishery.

"A few fish and a few fishermen," said Mike emphatically. "I mean, there are probably only a few hundred steelhead in this run."

Given his extensive experience on the tributaries of the lower Skeena, Mike is in as good a position as anyone to make this call. As we had convincingly demonstrated that morning, these cold, hard steelhead had only a few places—small, white-water pockets and a few suitable tailouts—to hide. For a pair of privileged anglers willing to withstand the rigours of finding them there is wonderful sport, but there aren't enough fish to give a lot of fishermen good fishing.

With the exception of the Lakelse, Copper and Kitsumkalum the rivers flowing into the last hundred miles of the Skeena have narrow valleys which see lots of rain and little sunlight. These are tough, Spartan environments for fish, which explains the scarcity of resident trout. Even in their pre-contact state it's unlikely that these rivers had populations of fish anywhere near as large as those swimming up the rivers of southern BC, Washington, Oregon, and California.

After lunch we spent a few more hours fishing then made a leisurely run up the river to Alastair Lake. When it comes to geography the Gitnadoix is the odd river out among the lower tributaries of the Skeena. Its lower seven miles are characterized by fast, narrow, rocky stretches and plenty of bends. The upper 12 miles of river are calm and flat, meandering through a wide valley filled with swamp and beaver ponds.

I asked Mike about the fine cutthroat fishing the swampy section of river is reputed to have. I was knocking on the wrong door. Mike fishes steelhead almost exclusively. He'd never sampled the area.

We passed Maygar Creek, and a rock bluff where we counted a dozen goats. The river was braided. Mike took all the right channels.

"What about the lake?"

Mike shook his head as we picked our way through the logs that had been pushed and pulled to the west side of the lake by wind and the gentle draw of the river.

"Too cold. I've heard there are a few Dolly Varden. They probably follow the creek sockeye that spawn in the feeder creek at the far end."

Mike Whelpley on the Gitnadoix early in the year.

I'd heard of these sockeye, unique in that they don't turn red, even in the latter stages of spawning.

Alastair was at the bottom of a large granite bowl made up of steep mountains sloping down to water level. There were no beaches. We skirted the lake, past a half sunken trapper's cabin that Mike thought may have belonged to Kolbjorn Eide, then headed back down river. At the base of the steeper slide chutes mounds of ice and snow lay glistening in the river.

"Jackie and I camped here one time," said Mike pointing out a clearing that lay opposite a wide chute polished by frequent slides. "We got up in the morning. After breakfast, we broke camp and went downstream a mile or so to fish. Slides were coming off. We didn't think much about it until the water came up and big chunks of ice came floating down the river. 'There's something wrong,' I said to Jackie. We drove upriver to check things out and there was our camping—or what was our camping spot—buried in 20 feet of snow. A slide had come down right across the river and covered it."

"It's a good thing your breakfast wasn't more leisurely," I said.

In the narrow valleys of the lower Skeena the weather is moody. By the time we set up camp at the top of the fast water the mountains were obscured by low gray clouds. It began to drizzle. Mike fished in the twilight while I wrote in my diary by flashlight. The fire was still glowing when we fell asleep, aided by the soft, stress-free fatigue that follows a day of pleasant exertion.

Morning Day Two: We were roused by rain pelting down on the tent. It was shivery. Mike was ebullient. "A bump of water will bring the fish in," he said, as I shielded my coffee from the downpour. When it comes to steelheading, Mike is seldom wrong. The river had risen and was still rising when we reached the Tallywhacker. We did well, Mike much better than I, which I attributed partly to his superior skill, partly to the fact he was float fishing while I stuck to the fly, and partly because I'd torn a hole low down in the leg of my waders, necessitating frequent trips to shore to drain the water and shake the circulation back in my left leg.

I looked up. Clouds scudded frantically north over the mountains, yet besides the rain there were no symptoms of a storm within the walls of the Gitnadoix Valley.

By afternoon I was shaking with cold. "You all right?" asked Mike. Then, before I could answer he suggested we leave. " You don't want to get hypothermia," he said.

Reluctantly we left the fish behind. I hunkered down in behind the bow of the boat to get out of the wind. Mountaineers have told me the trip down is always more dangerous than the trip up. For river boaters the trip out is always more dangerous than the trip in. At several points I held my breath as Mike slithered through a tricky turn. When we squirted out into the Skeena the wind was howling. It looked like an angry sea. Mike guided the boat over the six-foot waves hollering like a cowboy busting broncos, while I peered over the bow and shook.

We took out at the Exchamsiks. The storm had passed. All along Highway 16 trees were down. At the approach to the Kalum River bridge a trio of cottonwoods had fallen across power lines.

"Must have been some kind of storm," observed Mike.

"Some kind of storm" was an understatement. We later discovered that while we were intercepting Gitnadoix steelhead a vicious southeaster had whipped in from the Douglas channel sinking small craft caught unawares, blowing over large tracts of forest, inflicting all kinds of damage. A chopper, probably out to survey the damage, whirred by overhead. Mike looked up, "Ah, the ultimate toy," he sighed.

Lax Ghels: River of Clams

Spring Fishery: Geometry and Cutthroat Trout

Lines and circles: a series of short lines formed an arc across the hard wood decking of the bridge. The evening sun flickered through the spars. Below the Skeena was gray and swollen, running curves and lines to the sea: linear but actually part of a cycle, like the straight running, cyclic salmon that will run hard against it after the water has dropped some and summer has begun.

It was the month of the greenest greens in the seasonal cycle. The wheels rattled against the decking of the bridge then hummed on the asphalt of Queensway. After the hill we sped along the road to the lake. The tires spat gravel, a cloud of dust spewed out behind us. The tarmac at the airport stretched out in a straight line to the east.

We parked in the place where, not so long ago, the distances were obscured by dense forest. Now that the old trees are gone, the landscape stretched before us like quilted prairie—polygons; a next generation is starting to poke out between stumps and fireweed. We take some comfort from that.

There were a few turns. The bridge across the creek had been swept aside by last fall's freshet, but except for that, the trail was the same as it was last season and the season before.

We arrived at the river. Finlay started in immediately. I sat on a stump and watched flycatchers dart above the riffles. An osprey flew downstream and landed on a branch. I watched him for a while then looked away. When I looked back, I saw the splash then watched him rise from the river with a fish in his talons, predator and prey. That cycle started me thinking about time and progress and the linear way modern man defines history. I wondered whether we haven't made a serious mistake in seeing progress as a continual march of technological advancement: there must be great risk in moving away from natural directions.

Mayfly nymphs had been stirring along the bottom all evening; some had begun the first part of their perilous drift downstream. Long shadows stretched out over the river. The wind dropped.

Caddisflies darted upstream, as they always do. Some bounced off the surface of the river. The trout have seen this all before with their ancestral eyes. They hovered over the bottom, occasionally rising gently to intercept drifting nymphs.

A white black bear or kermode. The symbol of Terrace, B.C. Myron Kozak photo.

The mayflies reached the next stage in their reproductive cycle. I looked up through the light drizzle and saw pale olive duns rising through it. The oblique light illuminated them. The river erupted with trout and whitefish, rising, deadly and accurate, to intercept hapless duns.

It was time. I slipped into the river and caught one of the ephemeral insects to confirm that my imitation was close enough in colour and size. I cast a straight line then threw a curve upstream.

I held my watch close to my face; eleven o'clock. A pair of mergansers, stretched taut, flew like darts upstream. It was a full moon. The extra light would give us a few more minutes on the stream. I cast around for the largest rise, then cast a curved line toward it. It was 20 feet away. After three casts and three drifts, I made a convincing presentation. Up he came, head and eye, a silver flank, a broad tail. I moved to match his smooth and deliberate rhythm with a measured sweep of the rod. I had him. Though he fought well—straight vertical lines at sharp angles, his body an arc one way, then another—the struggle was more work than pleasure. A handsome fish, he filled the net.

The hatch was short. By eleven-thirty it was all over save for a few isolated rises. "Can't see my fly anymore," I said to Fin. The beam from his flashlight bent against the surface. Its reflection highlighted the spreading circles of a rise.

We waded cautiously through the shadows. Straight lines of light from our flashlights illuminated the trail. Moonlight flooded the landscape. As we put the rods in the car the call of geese echoed down the valley, another one of the circles that spin around us continually.

"Canada geese, " said Fin looking to the sky. "It's nice to hear them again."

A Giant at Mid-River

His head was enormous, much larger than I'd thought. We'd been close a few times, though it was never our intention to be. The first time, I saw his wake in the alders, a green wave moving through the brush like the kind a summer wind sometimes makes, but concentrated, accompanied by the snap of dead branches, and the rush of leaves brushing against something substantial.

It was July, early in the month. Everything was growing wildly, sucking up energy in the long sunlit days. Everything was green and dense. Skunk cabbage overflowed the swamps. Ferns, only a few weeks ago fiddle scrolls poking through the damp ground, were now taller than a tall man. The huckleberry bushes were heavy with fruit, which, I suspect, was why he was there.

I was there for trout and char. After a sweaty struggle against the resistant brush, I felt the river owed me a few good fish. It was just after I rounded the first bend, wading upstream, concen-

Deer. Myron Kozak photo.

trating on the fly drifting downstream, that I saw the wave moving away from me. I didn't know the engine of that phenomenon then, but I knew from its purposeful motion it was not frightened, simply moving instinctively. It made me shudder.

His claws are long, worn at the tips, extending from paws as big as pie plates.

I'd seen tracks in the area before—at Gledhill's, along the Moose Run, near White Creek. Big prints, filled with water, sunk deep in the sand, once beside a grotesque male humpback, the fish twitching, blood oozing from the gaping wound where its back was bitten off. That time I glanced furtively upstream. The upturned roots of a fallen spruce blocked my view. The coho could stay in the stream, I decided, then I took the trail back to the truck.

His coat is thick and dark, without lustre now that the powerful muscles behind it are no longer taut, filled, animated by blood pumped from that great heart.

His dark coat was a prominent feature the last time we almost met. It was fall, early fall, with the leaves staring to turn. I was only a few feet from the place where I'd first felt that mysterious presence. I'd been swimming minnows under banks and logs. A pair of fat harvest trout had smacked the fly and sizzled when they took to the air. I followed the sweep of the line until it hung directly below me, and there, further downstream, I saw him. At first I thought he was a stump. He moved. I made the connection between spoor, the force that had moved the trees, and him. He was the size of a buffalo. He was magnificent, moving with the confident motion of an animal accustomed to moving with abandon, scattering lesser creatures before him. He didn't know fear. At that moment I did. The sight of him—all that power. Fear battled fascination. In the end I was fixed, motionless, staring at the giant hump-backed animal whose size made him appear even bigger than he was.

He rooted about in a log jam, looking for a fish carcass, then moved off with motions too fluid and graceful for a creature so large. There was a time, not long ago, when giants like him were one of many; it had to be that way on a river that still supports a million salmon each year.

Here we are, meeting for the last time face to face now. His bulk and lack of fear were his downfall. He stood out clearly crossing a clear cut. When the pickup roared up, so did he. The shot was an easy one, even though the trigger man was out of focus from the liquor he'd been drinking as he hunted the roads from within the comfort of the cab.

Now the great grizzled bear is out of place, filling the box of the pickup with his bulk—not ferocious anymore with his huge head draped over the tailgate. He'll take down no more moose, yank no more salmon from rivers, swagger over no more slide chutes in spring, dig no more cabbage from the bottom lands, tear apart no more berry bushes.

The Skeena below Kitwanga. Mike Whelpley photo.

His death will be commemorated by a line in Boone and Crocket. His carcass might be made into a rug. Or, maybe he'll be mounted in a ferocious pose. Taxidermists—even the best of them—won't be able to capture a shadow of his terrible magnificence.

Armistice Day

The eleventh day of the eleventh month found me rattling over the pitted logging road to the Lakelse River in a depressed state brought on by the remembrance of Hiroshima, the Holocaust, and the wars that took my grandfather to the fields of France—where he inhaled the gas that weakened and ultimately killed him—and my father to Holland, where he helped liberate my mother's people from the Nazis.

To teach the children in my class why the poppies they wear are more than lapel decorations, I'd read them excerpts from a book on the Jewish genocide: a child's garden of horrors called Smoke and Ashes. It was written in clear, direct prose, which made it all the more disturbing. More disturbing to me than to my young charges, I suspected, because their distance from it is greater.

I stopped on the bridge. There was nobody there. The river was clean. I noticed that the towering cottonwoods that formerly stood along the south side of the river were gone I wondered if they'd be made into crates for Japanese motorcycles. The last of their yellow leaves, shaken loose by cold fall winds, should have been rattling through the rib cages of those sentinels now. I recalled the sound.

It was the last time I would find myself fishing the big northern coho of the Lakelse alone. Only the weekends attracted fishers then, and not many of them. The preferred method of anglers then was casting lures: spinners and spoons. Doug Webb was the first Skeena fisher to solve the riddle of bringing Lakelse coho to the fly.

A home-grown fisherman dedicated to fly fishing, Webb had spent many frustrating days trying to persuade Lakelse coho to bite a fly. During this process, he noted that the fish rushed into the lower river in large schools. The water was almost always low and clear. The fish were wary, many were snagged, only a few bit. Webb reasoned a small fly would not spook the salmon. He was right they didn't scatter but they didn't rise to the fly drifting above their heads either. Getting a size eight Teal and Silver to the right depth was difficult. Webb patiently spliced lengths of sinking lines with different sink rates together until he found a hybrid line that was reasonably pleasant to cast and would sink deep enough to interest coho. After that, the fly, at least as fished by Doug Webb, proved to be the best way to catch Lakelse northerns.

The coho were fresh, rolling frequently when I waded into the long pool below the logging bridge. A frequent fishing partner, Webb had shared his secrets with me. I had a facsimile of his hybrid line on my reel. The line cast well, something impossible to do with the fast sinking leaden lines that would later make fly fishing the method of choice for Lakelse coho.

The fish were concentrated in the tail of the run. I found a nice male there, a good fish of about 12 pounds. Coho do not usually leap, but they run hard and fast. This one did. I dispatched him, made my way up the bank to the truck, then drove off looking for changes.

Lakelse Main had not seen much traffic for some time. Water from the beaver ponds lapped at its shoulders. A new creek was cutting a new bed into the road near the power line. I accelerated so as to avoid getting mired in the soft gravel of the shoulder. Around the next bend an entire hillside had been razored and burned—more smoke and ashes. No band of trees had been left along the roadside to soften the view of the charred remains and the red earth. Empty bottles of chain saw lubricant lay beside the road.

On the north side of the roadway black, hollow stumps reminded me of the cedar swamp that once stood there. I wondered at the logic that leads men to cut trees of negligible value to the mill but of inestimable value to the creatures of the marsh and systems it feeds. I remembered a winter day when a big bull moose led Mike and me on a moose chase over the snow crust and iced ponds of that swamp.

There were few coho at Gledhill's. But, it didn't matter. I was after cutthroat. I found them throughout the pool. Not big fish, but nice fish. The Moose Run flows from Gledhill's. Before it takes a sharp bend, it runs toward a steep, tree covered mountain. I wondered how long it would be before it too is covered in scars.

I followed Lakelse Main past White Creek. More new logging—god they cut quickly nowadays—another tortured landscape brought on feeling of intense loss. On the river below Mink Creek, I saw light through the trees where before it was dark and green. The view started me thinking about the Bell-Irving, of No Gold Creek, the Clore and Skeena West, and I wondered how many riverscapes would be memories next year. I wondered if someday soon there will be no more Remembrance Days because there will be nobody to remember.

The Lakelse is unique among the rivers flowing into the lower Skeena. Warmed and nurtured by geothermal springs scattered around the shores of Lakelse Lake, the river supports a diversity of wildlife greater than any of the rivers feeding the last 100 miles of Skeena. Lax Ghels to the native peoples, the river of clams was so bountiful a waterway that coastal tribes annually endured the long paddle from tide water to the upper river where they set up fish camps, harvested berries, and stripped bark for baskets and boxes from the giant, sinewy cedars along the river's corridor.

Amazed by the abundance of sea-run and resident cutthroat, Rocky Mountain whitefish and Dolly Varden char, the first white settlers dubbed it "Trout River". It's hardly surprising that trout thrive in the river whose name was later bastardized to "Lakelse" since in strong years over a million pink salmon will plug the river, enriching the ecosystem with eggs, and flesh in the fall, and spawn silvery hordes of out-migrant fry to run a gantlet of cut-throat, rainbow, Dolly Varden and whitefish each spring.

A robust run of the Skeena's largest coho surge up the Lakelse through the reflections of yellowing cottonwood trees, and a modest run of Chinook and a small run of sockeye move into the system in summer as well. Three distinct races of steelhead—early run winter fish, a small population of summer-run fish and the large, strong run of winter fish—use the river.

Like many of the valleys on the Lower Skeena, the Lakelse has had most of its forest cover removed through a process of strip mining inaccurately called harvesting by foresters. That the river has managed to retain much of it riches is testimony to how remarkably rich it was, as well as a function of the natural durability it retains thanks to its gradual gradient and the amount of spongy swampy land next to it.

As is so often the case, logging roads have provided relatively easy access at the expense of fish and game. The grizzlies that cross mountain ranges in search of salmon and berries are becoming increasingly rare. There are far fewer black bears, fewer moose and fewer fish.

Because they are biters, Lakelse steelhead give the false impression of abundance. Radio tagging studies and creel censuses have dispelled this myth. One fall steelhead was caught by

Skeena summer steelhead. Myron Kozak photo.

Terrace guide Stan Doll. After having a transmitter rammed down its gullet and two tags punched into its hide, it was released only to be captured again seven times. The seventh fisher smacked the creature across the skull then returned the transmitter to the Fish and Wildlife Branch in order to reclaim a fifty dollar reward. Though no other tagged steelhead displayed such strong suicidal tendencies, recaptures were frequent. It is not surprising that better access to this small population of fish by a growing population of resident and foreign fishers has greatly reduced the ratio of fish caught to angler effort.

More insidious, and potentially much more destructive to the Lakelse system, is the problem of ruralization. This is a process whereby land supposed to be part of the forest land base in perpetuity (as well as land whose designation is unclear) mysteriously becomes available to hobby farmers or families looking for full or summertime residency near water. As more and more people encroach upon precious wetlands, invaluable nurseries for salmonids are ruined.

To make matters worse, flooding, exacerbated by logging and global warming trends, floods the driveways and basements of the people who had no business building on flood plains in the first place. When the water fills their basements these folks run to the provincial government, hands extended and demand compensation for their foolishness in the form of hair-brained dredging schemes, dikes and dough.

The Lakelse still affords an angler glimpses of trumpeter swans, osprey, eagle, all manner of water fowl, bear and moose. Otters can still be seen rooting around in the calm beds in the summer and sliding on icy banks in winter. The possibility of catching salmon, steelhead, char, whitefish and trout on a day's outing is still possible, but the magic of the river hangs by a thread.

War Games: The Green River

Just when sweet visions of green, aromatic woods and fry-filled, ice free shallows were dancing through our heads like mayflies mating in a spring breeze, a cold front swept down from the pole and we slipped back into a winter coma. Ice anchored itself to the rocks and the river banks tightened up once again, Oh cruel twist of fate, when the rivers such a short time ago seemed so pregnant with piscatorial possibility!

"When is the best time to go fishing?" asked the famed angler and philosopher, Roderick Haig-Brown, rhetorically. "When you can," was his answer. Heeding that advice, Webb and I struck out across the recently brittle, now rock hard crust of snow to the lower Kalum River, our 15-foot, two-fisted rods rasped against the alders.

When we arrived at the river, it was flowing, but only just. Big chunks of newly hatched ice bobbed downstream. Slush curdled on the bottom. We shrugged our shoulders and, at my suggestion, made for the truck. From there we drove to Highway 16 and headed in the direction of Prince Rupert. My logic: the weather will get milder as we near the coast. Webb, having heard many a hairball idea from me before, looked skeptical, but lured by the spirit of adventure, he
agreed.

It was cold, clear, and sunny. Larger chunks of ice than those we saw on the Kalum were shuttling back and forth with the tide. Miserable eagles sat in the trees, patiently waiting for the eulachon to appear. We stopped at the Green River. A young fisher from Prince Rupert told me a few months earlier that the river had steelhead. We knew there was a run of fall coho, and there may also be trout. The river was mud brown and beginning to freeze. I suggested that it might be flowing upstream.

A short way up the logging road, spring had begun. We followed a set of wolf tracks to the first clear cut. More and more people are using the woods now. In the fall there is evidence of mushroom hunting, hiking and bird watching. In the winter there are snow machine tracks, but here, a mile up the valley of the Green, Webb and I came across evidence of a new and bizarre outdoor recreation, one rooted firmly in the darker and deadlier recesses of time.

"North Coast War Games" proclaimed a large sign set in the middle of a logging slash. This is appropriate, I thought, what with the place looking like it's been hit by squadrons of bombers.

Scattered throughout the area were crudely thrown together shacks on stilts. Headquarters for the opposing forces. I remember reading about the characters who run around in catchy camouflage clothing, shooting each other with paint filled pellets.

With the conflagration in Kuwait ongoing, this remnant battle scene in the midst of a clear-cut no man's land seemed particularly absurd. Bang...bang...splat...yer dead! Another paint splattered warrior bites the newly exposed forest floor.

We imaged ersatz commandos arguing over who will play Norman Schwarzkopf and who will be the dastardly Sadam. The mind boggles at the opportunities for technological expansion for the weekend warriors: dud scuds filled with interior latex; tiny tiger tanks capable of volley after volley of watercolour; Apache helicopters bristling with egg tempera smart bombs—state of the art ballistics for the mother of all phony wars.

We left the war zone, continued a short way then made our way through the trees to the river. Still life. It was frozen. The ice crystals on the stream side glinted in the sun. A grouse hooted from somewhere in the thicket. Webb and I drank steaming tea, and thought about spotted cutthroats chasing slim, silver-bodied flies through these tea coloured waters.

Insect Creek

Bad water chased us out of town. Clay from Mink Creek was bleeding into the Lakelse, truncating the river, covering our favourite spring steelhead water in the process. The Zymoetz should be clear as air in April, low and cold and full of spooky fish, some old, a few new. But it wasn't. It hadn't been clean since the year before last. Another clay slide was the culprit, one opened up by high water caused by rain on snow and aggravated by the removal of the forest cover. "Higher highs and lower lows," Bob Clay, the Kispiox guide, likes to say. "That's what happens when you mow too much of the forest in a watershed. You've got the same amount of water, but the highs are higher, the lows are lower."

These high waters aren't very kind to log jams either, pushing them up to and over the banks, far out of the reach of the fish who use them in much the same way people use apartment blocks and grocery stores. It's sad, but spring is no time to be sad; it's a time for optimism; days are getting longer and warmer. It's a time to think of trips.

My idea this spring was to explore a creek that feeds the Skeena up country. Kenny Downs told me about it two years ago. Lots of steelhead he said. I swapped him some flies for a

Judge Paul Lawrence and Dease.

Skeena

Seven Sisters Mountains and the Skeena River. Myron Kozak photo.

sweatshirt with Saturday Night Blues and CBC emblazoned across the front. Kenny tried them on the creek without success, but then he's inexperienced with the fly. "It's worth a look-see," I told Webb. He agreed to go, but reluctantly. I don't blame him, after all we've chased wild geese on spring weekends in the past.

The chosen day was vivid. The Seven Sisters stood out in bold relief against a blue cloudless sky. "Looks like there's more than seven," observed Webb. "More like nine or ten." I counted. It seemed there were more than seven spires to me too. "Maybe the guy that named them was more concerned with alliteration than accuracy," I said, "a fan of sibilance."

The road ended at a store marked "Store", nothing more. Bibelots sat shoulder to shoulder on the sills, a rusted old mailbox, newly sawn wood waiting for splitting, canned goods on counters, graying walls, a cedar roof; nobody home. I knocked to confirm it. We began packing gear into back packs for the walk along the tracks when one of those trucks that run on rails pulled up on the siding. Out jumped a man with long hair on the sides and no hair on top. His coveralls were greasy, his shoes were greasy. His truck was too. Webb asked him what he did. He took his thick glasses off, wiped some grease from his eyebrows, then told us he was greasing the rails. I thought they were plenty slippery already, but didn't want to spend precious exploratory time asking then listening to the explanation, so I remained quiet.

Webb fished for a ride. The greaser was obliging, but headed the wrong way: home, Prince George where, he said, he'd set out on the grease trail weeks ago. Before he left he warned us of two imminent trains. "We'll hear them," I said. "You might not hear these ones in time," he said, ominously.

Water rushed out of the hills. The sweet smell of the woods mixed with the odour of railway ties baking. The trains, as we had been warned, approached quietly. They hummed, sang against the tracks, some cars whirred, sounded like the papery wings of giant dragonflies. Three miles felt like six.

Some creeks are rivers, this one was a creek. We awkwardly crawled around the canyon at its mouth. At one point all the water pushed powerfully through a spot no more than four feet wide. When we were past the rock gates we found a flood plain as wide as the canyon was narrow—wide and shallow with no water that promised fish.

Compressed packs of snow lined the banks. Another mile, another canyon. This one was wider enclosing a pool. A well manicured trail ran along one side. At two points along it someone had constructed benches, well built and well used. Above the canyon the river contours mirrored the reaches we'd just passed. "I'll bet my waders this is where Kenny found those fish," I said to Webb. "There's nowhere else for them to hide," he answered.

We fished. There wasn't much to fish, and we covered it well.

Zero. Too early, we realized, but there would be fish there soon. I looked at the fire pit in front of the benches. Here was a place a dad could bring his son, help the boy catch a fish, then show him how to kill it. That done, the boy could pack the fish home. He could show it his mom. He'd be swelled with pride. She'd cook it well and the family could dine on it, commenting on the sweetness of the flesh, and on how well the boy had done to catch such a handsome creature. I'm sure dads have used this place for this purpose. It was the ideal spot for it. It was nice to know such places still exist.

Khyex River: Two Tries

Our first trip to the Kyhex was my idea, I admit. When we arrived at the river's mouth some thirty miles east of the Prince Rupert, the tide was out. Webb deftly flipped the canoe up and onto his shoulders, slipped his neck in the yoke and trotted down the bank to the river. He insists on doing this himself, which is just fine with me.

With the river spread out all over the tidal flats there was no opportunity to paddle. Webb pulled a length of rope from his pack, fastened one end to the bow and the other to the stern. With the current keeping the boat away from our feet, we plodded upstream, making sucking sounds as we pulled our boots free of the muck with each step.

After two miles of trekking through the mud the valley narrowed. We hopped in the canoe and paddled for short stretches until the valley became steeper again. We were relieved to be able to stay in the boat.

The architecture of the valley was typical, even more breathtaking than the other rivers feeding the lower Skeena; magnificent stone walls at their best in the cool, fragrant, clear air of spring. We stopped paddling to look upward. At one point an avalanche roared out of the distance and shot over a high precipice sending snow and rock cascading into the valley. Except for the places where just such an event had left some large rocks in the river it was sandy. Ideal places, we agreed, for fall coho.

The current wasn't strong, but strong enough to strain our arms. "At least we'll have the river with us on the way," said Webb to provide some relief. We moved on hoping to find the rock-filled runs that steelhead prefer around each of the many bends—five miles, 10 miles, still nothing of the kind.

When a morning's paddling was behind us, the roar of white water reached our ears. Happily there were no falls, just a long cataract. We beached the craft next to the pool at the foot of the rapids. It fished well, giving us a trio of hard, bright steelhead: small fish that had not been in the valley much longer than we had. We looked at the brush-filed banks with trepidation, thankful that the going would be easier since the sun had had little time to penetrate the narrow valley and set the frustrating undergrowth growing. Still, the hike through swamps filled with devil's club, willow and alder was demanding. We walked miles, and there was still no end to the cataract, and worse still, no pools

Seven Sisters at dusk. Myron Kozak photo.

promising fish. Webb checked the time. We had only one day, and needed to catch the tide. We turned back reluctantly with thoughts of miles and miles of fine steelhead water that may lie above the chute.

The paddle downstream was glorious. We stopped at a rustic, but well built, cabin at the mouth of Arden Creek. I flipped through a diary the proprietor had left on the table. Entry after crudely penciled entry recorded catches of coho and steelhead and bear sightings. It was if we were explorers who had set out to charter unknown frontiers and serendipitously come across the journal of a party that had gone on before.

The tea coloured flow of Arden Creek was substantial. It reminded me of streams on the Queen Charlotte Islands—in fact, if it had been on the Charlottes it would have been a river, a destination river whose runs of fish would be eagerly anticipated by a dedicated fishery. It was all we could do to tear ourselves away from it, but it was mid-afternoon. We had to move.

Giant spring decomposing in the shallows at the German Bar on the Skeena River.

When we arrived at the tide mark the broad braided trickle had become a sea. A sharp wind had moved up the estuary with the tide. We rowed harder than we had on the trip in, made slow headway. "It's a law," Doug declared, "When you're paddling a canoe the wind is always in your face."

The diary entries, and the realization that the tides severely limit jet boat access brought us back in the fall. Webb had bought a jet driven inflatable. I bought a book of tide tables, and we set out on a day filled with drizzle. There were coho, but not nearly as many as we'd expected. Like the Khasiks and the Exchamsiks, the relatively gentle current of the river's lower floors were kind to the fly. With no reason for a heavy line it was still possible to fish with grace.

Arden Creek proved difficult. After mooring the boat, we walked and waded upriver, in the few spots were it was possible to cross. Deep, dark pools punctuated riffles too shallow to hold fish. Despite the frequent snags, the river was a gear fisher's dream; for the fly it was awkward. There were cutthroat with the salmon, though, enough of them to save the day.

Tired and scratched up by brush, we arrived at the confluence of the creek and the river to discover that the tide had retreated leaving most of the inflatable high and dry. We rushed across the

stream and pushed, and twisted the boat from side to side, moving it by inches but moving it. "No time to stop," said Webb breathing heavily, "the tide's still running." It was raining harder. My raincoat was a sponge. It took over an hour of rocking and rolling, but to our immense relief the boat came free saving us from a wet miserable night.

The Khyex, we decided, is simply too much work for a short trip. A week and a full camp were needed to do it justice.

Large Salmon, the Sport of Kings

It was a hot, languorous day. Veteran Skeena salmon guide, Stan Doll was anchored close to the Island, working a favoured slot he'd found after years of trial and error. The fishing was decent. The water was good. There was no need for bait. The Skeena offered three feet of visibility. Early in the afternoon, Stan helped his German sport kill a 30-pound Chinook.

The heavy current hissed against the bow of the boat. The rods bobbed rhythmically, in time to the whirring lures anchored a long cast below the stern. Stan and the German took off their shirts, ate sandwiches and drank beer. The German, a doctor, told Stan of the Old World and of his appreciation of the New in fluent English.

Dinner time passed. There was still plenty of fishing time left, but both men were hungry. Stan checked the pulsing rod tip for the hundredth time then glanced at his watch. 8:30. He put on his shirt, the first move toward home, when the rod bent violently.

"I believe you have one!" yelled the German.

The old Silex reel growled angrily. Thirty pound test nylon peeled from the drum. Stan leapt up. The rod bent deeply. Line sizzled through the water. In his career Stan had landed many large salmon—some well over 60 pounds—the muscles in his back told him this was one those.

Despite its large capacity, there was not enough line on the Silex; for Chinook giants there seldom is. At Stan's command the German brought up the anchor. The boat started downstream, pushed by the current, pulled by the salmon.

Thirty minutes after hook up, the fish still fought deep. Stan gauged its dimensions by the arc of the rod, the tension on the line, the duration of the struggle and distance they had traveled downstream. The struggle wore on, out of sight of competing fishermen now, a mile below the Island. The great fish began to show some signs of fatigue. Stan gained a little line, lost it, then pumped the rod gaining more than he'd lost the first time.

The salmon breached, too far away for a good look. Stan's arms ached. He was gaining. The rod hummed. The line hummed, as they drifted around yet another broad bend of the river and over another riffle. The fish rolled once more. This time both men got a glimpse of him.

"It's the size of a seal," Stan yelled to the German.

The doctor was so impressed he forgot his English and babbled to himself in his mother tongue.

The fish rolled to the surface once more, then streaked for a log jam at the lying off the mouth of the Lakelse River. Stan tried to break its run by jamming his palm against the outside of the old reel. His hand burned. The fish bore on. He reached the jam. The line stopped.

The German shook his head from side to side vigorously, mumbling something in German. Stan knew only a few words of German, but he recognized the international tone of despair. The line wasn't moving. Stan pulled then pulled again, harder the second time. The line was unyielding.

"It's no good," he said.

"Ja, nicht gute."

Stan lifted the club he'd used to kill the smaller fish. With a circular motion he twisted the monofilament around it. He pulled. The line snapped. He gathered in the remains, then looked at his client.

"That fish could've gone a hundred pounds."

The German nodded. He had his fish. He had seen a Skeena giant, one of the world's biggest salmon—possibly a world record. Despite the disappointing finale, this had been a great trip. He had photographs to take home along with a grand tale of a grand fish.

Fly Fishing for Chinook, the Sport of Kings

In Alaska and the other American states with Pacific shores, *Oncorhynchus tshawytscha* is the king. In Canada his majesty shares the name Chinook with the dry wind that whips down from the Rockies bringing unseasonably warm air to autumn days. In Skeena he is the spring salmon, named for the time of year when the first of his numbers begin to appear in the river of the Kitsumkalums. Spring, Chinook, smiley, king—whatever you call him, he is the largest and strongest of the Pacific salmon with a prominent place in the dreams of sports fishers.

Like other fishermen, I'd caught springs with bait and lures, but sitting under the hot sun behind a forked stick watching a belled rod is more market fishing than fishing for sport. Casting spoons from one spot, though more sporting than still fishing, tends to be costly, and its still too sedentary a pursuit. For years I thought about bringing these leviathans to a fly. I had read plenty of articles about the exploits in Alaska, but these were invariably illustrated with pictures of fly fishers straining as they hoisted ripe kings the colour of fire trucks. Salmon guarding redds can easily be provoked to strike, but provoking them is like shooting nesting birds. No knowledgeable, ethical angler does it. No, the trick was to hook these fish when they were still clean and silver, new arrivals to fresh water.

In the summer of 1986 I set out after spring salmon in earnest. The first task was to assemble the right tackle for the job. Big fish demand big rods, I reasoned. In hindsight, I believe I should have purchased a tarpon rod, for the better leverage these poles have, but a ten weight, 15-foot Hardy Spey rod was hanging from the wall of the local sporting goods store. Because nobody in Terrace was using one at the time, and because this appealed to my iconoclastic nature, I bought it and very nearly wore my arms out trying to cast it in what I thought was the approved manner.

To complement the rod I purchased a Hardy Marquis, Salmon #3, a giant winch carrying a 40 yard double tapered fly line and hundreds of yards of backing its manufacturer claimed had a breaking strength of 30 pounds.

Mike Whelpley, who had been ramrodding the Kalum Project where some giant Kalum Chinook are taken each year for enhancement purposes, told me his crew had found a hulking male during a dead pitch, that even in its spent condition, weighed over 70 pounds. Firmly attached to the hinge of its toothy jaw was a number four Green Butt Skunk. So, in this anecdote was evidence that some Chinook will take a fly, and, given the size of the fish, a relatively small fly at that. I assembled an arsenal containing this pattern, a half dozen General Practitioners built on three and five ought Atlantic salmon hooks

Black bear cub dining on salmon. Myron Kozak photo.

as well as a number of two inch vinyl tube flies in Green Butt Skunk dress, but with a few thin strands of pearl Mylar lashed on under their polar bear wings. Since the regulations forbid trebles, I broke from the British canon and armoured them with needle sharp 2/0 bait hooks, choosing the red plated models in keeping with the red tail demanded by the recipe for Skunks.

The next hurdle was to find a spot where migrant Chinooks stacked up to marshal energy for the rest of their journey, excluding those spots where the current is simply too heavy for the fly. Unfortunately, Chinook often favour these heavy flows. I went through a list of rivers using a process of elimination: the Skeena was simply too big, the Chinooks, unlike their cousins, generally preferred to swim too far out in the river; the beaches of the Kalum, home of the biggest springs, were underwater during the peak migration of Chinook; it was the same situation on the Ecstall River; the Lakelse simply had too few fish—and most of the river was closed to fishing anyway. All of which left the Zymoetz. It, after all, hosted a strong run of springs, and, provided it wasn't too filled with glacial flour, had plenty of inside corners and long runs suited to fly fishing. Moreover, I remembered a day when Bill Burkland of Kitimat hooked a steelhead and a small Chinook on his six weight cane rod with a Muddler Minnow at the end of a floating line.

Finlay was skeptical. Gene Llewellyn downright disbelieving when I met them at Baxter's Riffle, showed them my outfit and told them my mission. It was a hot day. For the Zymoetz the water was clear, affording me two and a half feet of visibility. "If you stand in the river up to your knees and you can still see your feet, then it's fine for fishing," Finlay declared. "That's what Ted Rawlins used to say."

We didn't wait long for a fish to roll. I could see they were milling around where a strand of gravel lay at the tail of a rapid creating 50 yards of slower water behind it. The line was one of those fast sinking models, 12 feet long. I'd attached a short leader of 15-pound and one of Colonel Drury's Orange prawns. In short time I'd ambushed my first Chinook. It hit hard, setting off a large splash.

"We got one!" Gene yelled to Fin.

The fish proved to be about 15 pounds. There were no jumps, just strong determined runs. It was much stronger than a steelhead of the same size. "They're stronger, pound for pound," Gene agreed when I made this observation.

For a week I fished this ambuscade, beaching 12 salmon. The largest was the most memorable. A little over 50 pounds he pulled over half a mile from Baxter's to the Old Bridge. Twice he came within inches of spooling me, once running the backing all the way to the arbour knot. For all the excitement, there was something distasteful about the episode. The fish was on for an awfully long time before I could get him ashore. The fishing was more like work than sport. If I could somehow dissuade salmon of over 20 pounds from taking the fly, if the places to fish for them weren't so few, and the right conditions so hard to find, I'd still go out after them each summer.

Khatada: Misplaced Rainbows

Bill Gourlie is short, hard and wiry. The wind-burnished skin on his face is leathery and taut. Pronounced lines radiating from the corners of his eyes mark hours spent scanning valleys from rocky promontories, staring across the plains of places like the Spatsizi, glassing through hazy distances to greening slides and squinting down the barrel of a rifle. Bill's eyes are alert. Talking to him you get the feeling he's about to spot something at any moment and begin stalking it. Bill Gourlie's trophies attest to his mastery of the hunt. He is an endangered species, a trophy hunter.

I don't share Bill's passion for hunting because I've never hunted big game, and I was not brought up with it. But, because I hunt fish, I have some appreciation for his passion.

Bill is also a seasoned pilot. A few years ago he told me about a flight he'd made over the head end of a local watershed. The creeks, he said, were full of ripe salmon. Grizzlies, following their instincts, and the well worn trails of their ancestors, had lumbered down into the valley bottom to pull fish from the streams with their muscular jaws. "You shoulda seen them!" exclaimed Bill, emphasizing the point by making claw-like gestures with his shop worn hands. "I've never seen so many bears. Some of 'em were the size of buffaloes!"

Due to the thin protection of regulations, and, more importantly, miles of undisturbed timber, none of those bears were available to hunters. The fact that Bill was unable to put any of those bears in his sights didn't bother him; to know that they were there, to see them, was enough. A year later, Bill flew the same path. He was even more animated when he told me about that reconnaissance. "I saw some sows and a few two-year-olds, but not one big boar," he told me.

I asked his opinion, though I had a pretty good idea what he would say. "Poached," he shot back. And, it seems likely they were, for as Bill was quick to point out, a logging road snakes up the valley now. It wasn't the logging that hurt the bears, Bill argued, it was the improved access. Grizzly hides can fetch thousands of dollars, their viscera does too. That economic incentive combined with a conservation service made ineffectual by budgetary cuts, conspired to put the great bears in danger, according to Bill. He'd seen it all before.

Our shared concern for wildlife and my reputation as a fly fisherman, brought Bill Gourlie and me together the following spring. The season of growth is the best time for wildlife viewing; Bill's Super Cub was out of the hangar. He'd been prowling the Skeena Valley, noting changes and checking wildlife abundance.

One of Bill's favourite pursuits is setting his plane down on remote lakes and casting spinners from its floats. Khatada Lake, he told me, had been giving him some superb fishing. The trout had risen from the depths and were nearer

Blacktail deer. Myron Kozak photo.

the shallows. Bill was starting to think seriously about switching to the fly. I urged him on, drawing parallels between hunting trout and hunting game. As a result of this ongoing discussion, Bill asked me to come along and try for Khatada trout.

We lifted off from the slough behind his home at Old Remo and flew west. The day was clear, the mountains distinct. Bill started spotting game right away. "Moose," he'd call back over the roar of the engine. "Bear. Down there. By the power line." I missed the first few sightings then caught a fleeting glimpse of a bull moose before he disappeared into a thicket of red osier dogwood. I marveled at Bill's ability to sight animals from that height and at that speed.

Khatada has a number of falls and an imposing set of rapids barring access to fish to all but the lower mile of the river. I'd told Dionys deLeeuw, managing biologist for the Fish and Wildlife Branch in this region, and an expert of cutthroat trout, about the tales of uncharacteristically large trout to be had in Khatada Lake, some running to 10 pounds. Soon thereafter, Dionys made the trek up the river to sample the fish. The fish were large all right, but, surprisingly, they proved to be rainbows. Rainbow trout inhabit the more northerly lakes in Skeena. These fish, in a closed system so close to tidewater were anomalous. Perhaps the

Skeena steelhead. Myron Kozak photo.

Khatada cataracts, prior to some seismic event, were not as formidable as they are now enabling the progenitors of the few steelhead that still spawn in the lower river to reach the lake and the creek at the far end of it. The misplaced rainbows that now inhabit the lake may well be a cycle of steelhead trapped and forced to take up residence ages ago.

On our flight over the river we spotted some of these fish—salmon-sized fish, large enough to be clearly visible from the air—spawning at the outlet of the lake. Another aircraft was moored close by. A group of fishermen, either uninformed or unethical, were casting to them.

I judged the lake to be two miles long, a very deep bowl very similar to Alastair, but steeper. There were two cabins on it, large ones considering the effort it must have taken to get the building materials in. Bill thought one belonged to a commercial operation. Two fishers were trolling lures from tin boats driven by small motors, the way I understand the fishing is conducted on the lake for most of the year.

Sleeping Beauty Mountain overlooking Terrace, B.C.
Mike Whelpley photo.

As I looked for goats, Bill brought the plane down smoothly then steered it across the lake to a sandy beach. With the plane secured, he began casting a spoon far out into the lake. On the trip across I'd looked down. This was a deep lake. The first structure I sighted was an underwater cliff very close to shore. The success of Bill's lure and the plugs and lures favoured by the troll fishery strongly suggested that besides their genetic programming, the fish owed their size to the presence of bait fish, possibly kokanee. I knew bringing them to a fly was going to be a difficult proposition. I did my best, using a triangle taper floating line and a double haul to throw a silvery minnow imitation almost as far as Bill was pitching his lures.

Within an hour Bill had killed a three-pound fish—bright and firm, and definitely a rainbow. I did nothing. We drifted the plane to a log jam at the far end of the lake where I spotted some small fish hovering underneath the logs, but neither of us found fish there.

"You can't often do this," Bill said as he took the plane up the narrow valley of the creek feeding the lake from the south end. "Usually it's socked in with clouds." I looked at the walls of the canyon, dangerously close to the tips of the wings and understood what he meant. We climbed then banked sharply around a mountain peak and began our descent down the valley of Kadeen Creek into its sister valley, the Gitnadoix. Bill veered sharply west at the confluence of Kadeen and the Gitnadoix River. We were just above the tops of the trees. A large bear feeding in the swamp reared up on its hind legs as we flew by. "That's a big black," said Bill. In minutes we were moving north, up the Skeena, flying low over the bars. For Bill a normal outing, for me the day, fishless though it was, had been an exhilarating experience. My mind was filled with stunning landscapes, and images of fleeting game.

Oncorhynchus Nerka: A Pilot Fishery

Years ago, veteran conservationist and outdoor writer Lee Straight told me, there were so many Chinook, coho and steelhead around B.C. sportsmen didn't bother with the other species. At the request of the fishing industry, pink salmon and sockeye were designated commercial species by the Department of

Fisheries and Oceans without objections from sportsmen. The sockeye, since they have always fetched the highest price, are gold to what Lee calls the "market fishery."

In Skeena sportfishers were only concerned with sockeye in so far as the enhanced Babine River stocks attracted huge fleets comprised of fishermen from up and down the coast to the mouth of the Skeena where the indiscriminate methods they employed wreaked havoc with the less abundant sport fish stocks.

In the early days of the fishery the fleet moved far up the Skeena and fished until the paint peeled from their boats. Monitoring the landings the Federal Fisheries managers wisely realized that the fishery could not be sustained. Over time the fleets were regulated out of the river proper to the river mouth and what is now called Area Four, the approach waters to the Skeena. Though there were now time and location restrictions, advancements in technology ensured that the harvest remained at unsustainable levels. During some seasons as many as a thousand boats, many of them employing technologically superior equipment, mined the stocks with the predictable result that all races of anadromous fish save for the race of sockeye bred in spawning channels at Fulton River and Pinkut Creek on the Babine began to plummet.

The Skeena sport fishery was growing. Anglers working the river's mainstem noticed that the visible decrease in the number of fish rolling upstream coincided with the commercial openings at the river mouth. Veteran fishers angling the tributaries, except for 1986 when an as yet unexplained biological phenomenon brought a surprising number of steelhead back to the province's rivers, observed fewer and fewer steelhead and coho spawners each year. With summer coho the problem appeared to be particularly acute. Once so abundant in rivers like the Zymoetz, the small cohoes of July and August were downright scarce.

Led by indefatigable campaigners like former sport fishing ombudsman Jim Culp, the sportsmen of Region Six started organizing meetings, building organizations and lobbying in hopes of drawing attention to the plight of Skeena's sport fish and persuading politicians to force bureaucrats to in turn lean on fisheries managers to come up with adjustments, and ultimately, a restructuring of what had become an unwieldy, biologically offensive fishery.

As Lee Straight observed, during the span of his forty year career as an advocate for B.C.'s sport fish and sport fishermen,

Bulkley River float. Myron Kozak photo.

there has been a gradual change in attitude toward the sport fishing sector on the part of the Federal Department of Fisheries. At first, the opinions of sportsmen were ignored. Then came a time when they were tolerated, and grudgingly, listened to—though few of their suggestions were acted upon. Now, says Lee, it appears the opinions of sportsmen are being treated seriously, even solicited. Nowhere is this more obvious than in Skeena where, for the first time anywhere sportsmen, commercial fishermen and natives sit down, on a more or less equal footing, at the same table to receive information on the state of the fishery and then negotiate and, finally, make recommendations to the fisheries managers on how the fishery should proceed: a promising co-management process that may well be the shape of resource use decision making processes in the future.

Part of the initiative by Skeena sportsmen to save their sport fish led them to push for a pilot fishery for pink salmon and sockeye. The reasoning was straight forward. Pinks, though easy to catch, rely on abundance as a survival strategy. The Kispiox and Lakelse will host runs of over a million of these fish during years

German tourists prepare to attack the Skeena.
Myron Kozak photo.

of peak returns. Almost every small stream is used by humpbacks and the backwaters of the Skeena is plugged with them. Given this fact, there is no chance that sportsmen—especially since they are operating under a small bag limit—will deplete the runs. True, like the chum salmon, pinks tend to ripen quickly after they return to fresh water, but the fish available to anglers favouring the bars of the lower Skeena below Terrace are often in fine shape, many of them still carrying sea lice.

Skeena sockeye are also abundant, and they are notorious non-biters. You would expect that with all the lure fishers, bait soakers and fly casters fishing the Skeena each summer a good number of sockeye would have been caught incidentally; not so. Though anglers fishing the upper reaches of the Babine report that the same fish, red and ripe, bite so readily they are a nuisance, the same fish, when passing the portals of the lower Skeena, seem to have lock jaw. And, again, a limit of one fish per angler per day, advocates of the pilot fishery on the lower Skeena argued, would guarantee minimal impact on those fish.

Finally, sportsmen suggested to fisheries personnel that the possibility of catching a fish to eat—something that had been severely curtailed in recent years—would remove some of the

Coho fishing on the Kasiks River. Mike Whelpley photo.

⟡⟡⟡⟡⟡⟡⟡

pressure from steelhead and coho. Reluctantly, the DFO managers agreed to free up both those species on a trial basis to sportsmen, despite a deafening howl from the commercial fishermen, who, with a minimal understanding of the up river fishery, imagined hordes of sportsmen descending on the river to fill sacks with sockeye. The fishery has been a resounding success. Fishers who formerly employed bar fishing techniques pulled on waders and took to the water with lures and flies. Pinks came readily to the fly, as they always had done, though few anglers knew it, since only a few fished the big river with fly rods. The sockeye, as expected, continued to turn their noses up at almost everything shown them. Gradually, however, reports of small catches began to circulate as anglers discovered water where one was more likely to hook one of these silvery little torpedoes, and lures that caught their attention more readily.

Over a three year period, it became evident that the best catches were going to fly fishers, which led to increased sales of fly tackle and resulted in spin casters replacing the lures at the ends of their lines with flies. Veteran Skeena fly fisherman, Ed Chapplow was one of the first to solve the riddle of Skeena sockeye, and has caught them consistently and well since he unraveled that knot.

A former bridge and road builder and gentleman farmer, Ed's

experience fishing the lower Skeena spans more than three decades. He speaks fondly of bountiful days on the Lakelse and the Copper, where he learned how to fish the fly under the watchful eye of Ted Rawlins.

"I worked under Ted when he was a logging foreman in the Kalum Valley," Ed told me. "He was the best boss I ever worked for. He had a real feel for people. He fished the fly when nobody else was, back when the rivers were a lot different than they are now."

Different indeed: they ran clear and low during the cold winters that began in late November and ended in March, like winters in the Skeena Valley should. The heavy snow pack inland took months to melt in those days, keeping the Skeena high and gray for most of the summer. Fewer trailers, no need for subdivisions, fewer miles of river exposed, fewer fishermen, more fish, better fishing, Ted and his contemporaries were blessed, for sure.

Ed told of a time when the work was done early. Ted, knowing his young underling was fond of fishing, suggested the two of them go out after steelhead that afternoon. Eager for the opportunity to angle with an expert, Ed gathered up his gear and made for the Rawlins' small yellow house on Highway 16, a short distance from the Old Bridge.

"Jesus, I get out of the car with my spinning rod, and Ted looks at the pole. 'You're not going fishing with that thing?' he says." The way Ed told it, the question was more a command than a query.

"I told him it was the only rod I had. So, he goes in the house and comes out with a glass fly rod; it had a Hardy reel and a sinking line. Then he says, 'today you're going to fish with the fly.'"

Ed described driving up the Copper River to a pool just above the first canyon where Ted patiently showed him how to work out a short line.

"I caught two coho and my first steelhead on the fly."

Ed was securely hooked. Since that day, so many years ago, he has fished often, always with the fly.

According to Ed, Skeena sockeye, upriver fish with a few hundred miles of difficult water to negotiate before reaching the man-made spawning channels at Pinkut and Fulton, are almost always in motion. When they do rest it is only for minutes, and almost always at the foot of a shallow riffle, and that's where Ed fishes them. I spent the better part of a hot July afternoon watching Ed kill a sockeye, let another go and lose a large steelhead at the Ferry Island Riffle. He was using a fast sinking tip, the green line that used to be called "Hi-D" by the line manufacturers. At the end of the line he'd fastened a nine-foot leader, which I suspect he'd done to keep the fly riding above the tip of the line and, therefore, above the rocks. During the three hours I watched, Ed's hook never once caught a stone or stick, and there were many there.

Ed's sockeye was about five pounds, slightly larger than average. For a relatively small fish it fought impressively, making long runs and jumping three or four times. Ed played it gently, as if it were more fragile than, say, a steelhead, which, in effect, it was, for sockeye, since they feed exclusively on minute crustacea have no need for hard toothy jaws like their cousins. Having done it many times, Ed was careful not to pull the hook from the fish's soft mouth. It was a beautiful fish, with a bluish olive back, shimmering sides, an aquiline head, a small wrist and overall torpedo shape that had something to do with the ferocity of those long runs.

"A good scrapper," I commented as Ed dispatched the fish.

"Tasty too," Ed winked and pulled a kink out of the line.

And indeed it was. Later we ate steaks, red and rich with oil, and washed them down with cold beer underneath a clear blue sky as the birch and cottonwood leaves shimmered and rustled in a light and cooling summer breeze.

Kitsumkalum: Winter

Due to an enigmatic function of time and perception, the distance between winters seems shorter now than it did even a decade ago. Boyhood summers seemed to last years, now a two month span seems to whistle by in the time it takes to turn around. My father, who is now in his late seventies, tells me years are turned to months, months to days as a person ages. Such is the tyranny of time. Still, I take some comfort, none of it cold, in the fact that I share this affliction with everyone else, and I find myself actually looking forward to the cold season, as short as its months and days are.

In Skeena, winter is the season of monochrome and mist and flat light, a time when everything but time moves slowly through stiff landscapes. The river is lower, slower and muted. The surrounding land is silent for long periods, making the sounds that punctuate the quiet—the clatter of moose hooves over the cobbled bottom of a shallow riffle, or the wing beat and the fanfare of a flock of swans, or an ice shelf calving—louder and more startling.

There is an abrupt shift from the frantic tempo of fall, with its thrashing salmon, prowling bears and bickering birds, to the somnolent pace of the cold months. In winter there may be a few char, or a stray cutthroat trout to catch, but winter steelhead, rare, as hard as ice, with bellies as white as the snow and backs as gray as the leaden winter sky, are the true fish of winter. These are fish built for cold weather, not bottom fish but fish of the bottom—slow to bite, fighting the slow fight.

The Kitsumkalum is a good place to find winter steelhead. During summer the river has no beaches and its water is full of glacial flour, but when slashes of red and yellow begin appearing on the hillsides the water begins to drop gradually. By October the Culvert, Glacier Creek, Lone Cottonwood and a few lesser upper river runs are getting thinner. By November their bones are sticking out. By Christmas the water has cleared and the river is clearly defined.

In winter the summer steelhead that slipped into the system during the summer and fall months are distributed through the higher reaches of watershed, namely the Cedar and Beaver Rivers, Red Sand, Mud, and Kalum Lakes, and the ten or so miles of river above the two canyons. Joining them are newly arriving winter fish. Members of this pale race of stocky steelhead enter the river throughout the winter months. In fact, the spring run of Kalum steelhead are probably members of this same strain of winter run fish. As late as May a few of these brilliant creatures are still arriving.

Bait fishermen hunt the winter steelhead with 10-foot rods and single action reels, suspending salmon eggs or artificial lures beneath lead and a float in the traditional B.C. manner. It's a thrifty, effective way to fish and because of the extreme cold often encountered this technique was, save for still fishing from a perch near a fire, the only way to fish rivers like the Kitsumkalum.

Thanks to float fishing I learned a lot about the habits of the Kalum's winter steelhead. One year I beached over a hundred steelhead, more than half of which were pulled from the Kalum. All of the Kalum fish were subdued on a float rod. This kind of thing was overkill, I decided. Steelheading this way was just too easy. With the use of a balsa float I could drift my favourite lure, a gob of ersatz salmon eggs garnished with a tuft of chartreuse

Heavily spotted Lakelse steelhead. Mike Whelpley photo.

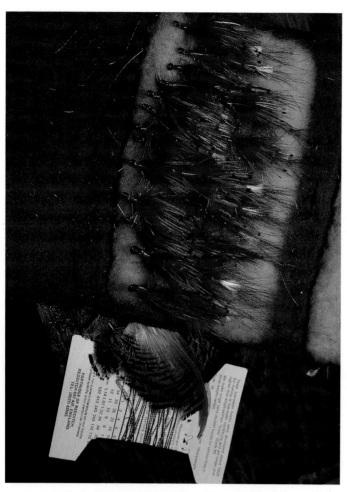

A flock of Orange General Practitioners ready for a winter assault on the Kalum River.

❦

yarn, into the most difficult of steelhead holding waters. More and more I missed the gentle and graceful exercise of fly casting.

British Columbia was British. It's hardly surprising, therefore, that the British techniques immigrated and were integrated into the angling praxis of its salmon-filled colony. Before they fell into disuse, two-handed cane rods were used by Bill Cunliffe and Tommy Brayshaw, to name two famous B.C. anglers, long before Art Lingren or anyone else picked up graphite models. Others claim to have stimulated the reintroduction of two-fisted fly rods to British Columbia, but Art was the first person I met, or read about, who used the double-hander for all his steelheading, and used it properly. I credit Art for making it possible for me to put down my bait pole and my cross-country ski poles and enable me to soldier out after winter steelhead with the fly rod.

Iced guides are a headache on winter days, even for the devotees of gear fishing. Line-borne water droplets are deposited on the guides during casting and retrieving. Eventually the water hardens into ice jams. On windy days the problem becomes acute. Fishers dipped and chipped and greased their line constantly. Things were even worse for fly rodders, who were forced to wave their rod back and forth in the chill air. Matters were further complicated by the small guides on fly rods and the fat line one needs to cast a fly. From Art I learned that once the line was free of the guides on a two-handed rod it didn't have to be shot or retrieved until a fish took hold. Here, then, was a technique that,

quite possibly, circumnavigated icing. That wasn't the only advantage to the long rod, according to Art. Not only could long lines be cast, he said, but—and this was the most important feature—much greater control could be exerted over its drift thanks to the luxury of length.

Hands exposed to water and wind are another painful problem associated with winter steelheading. Large single action casting reels of British manufacture eliminated the need to jam a gloved thumb into the cage of smaller multiplying reels, but working either type of winch with gloved hands was awkward and irritating at the best of times. When manipulating the long salmon rods there was no need to be winding the line in after each cast therefore thick woolen mitts could be worn all day without discomfort.

Because winter steelhead are reluctant to move any distance through frigid waters it is necessary to sink a fly close to the bottom. The smaller flies we fished in fall would work as well if they could be maneuvered to the required depths. We tried this, and though ugly leaden lines did take them down quickly, the flies remained there for only a very short time.

Doug Webb, with no knowledge of Bill MacMillan's experiments with the floating line in winter, had experimented with floating lines and heavy flies, arrived at some of the same conclusions, and adjusted his technique accordingly. Still, much Kalum water was resistant to that approach. A few of us waited patiently for the right weather conditions—and over the course of a winter there were seldom more than half a dozen days which fit the bill—then ventured forth in sub-zero temperatures with large, sparsely dressed patterns or heavily weighted dressings affixed to short leaders which were in turn attached to dense sinking tip lines. Sometimes, not often, we caught fish.

Hugh Falkus' book on salmon fishing gave me more hope. When used as intended, a very heavy fly could be thrown effortlessly thanks to the length of the pole and the mechanics of Spey casting, said Falkus. I was convinced. All that remained was to obtain a Spey rod and learn to Spey cast, both of which proved more difficult than I had anticipated.

After months of waiting, a 15-foot Hardy rod arrived at the local tackle store. The proprietor looked on skeptically, but happily, as I forked out 500 dollars for the rod, another 200 for a large salmon reel made by the same company, and another hundred for a 40-yard, 11-weight double taper line and backing. By day I took the gargantuan pole to a secluded bar on the Skeena and tried to make it work with the minimal instruction offered by Falkus' book. The last of the summer salmon surged by the tuft of fluorescent yarn I'd knotted to my leader unconcerned. At night I assembled large prawns, steelhead patterns on two and three ought hooks, and, taking another cue from the colour plates in Falkus' treatise, wound Green Butted Skunks around vinyl and copper tubes.

Overhead casting came quickly and effortlessly; if anything, casting a fly this way was easier than doing so with a shorter stick. The intricacies of the single and double Spey cast were a different matter. At the end of more than one session under the hot summer sun, my arms ached and my head throbbed. Lingren came to my rescue once again when he sent me a video of Falkus dancing the Spey Ballet. I slipped the cassette into the slot and watched, enthralled, as the master salmon fisher sent out long, looping arcs of line almost effortlessly. Now, at least, I had an idea of how the end result of the Spey cast should look. It is difficult to impart nuance on celluloid, however. I gained access to the intricacies of Spey casting thanks to a superb little manual called

34 Ways to Cast a Fly, which I unearthed in the sale bin of a second hand book store in Vancouver.

The book's author, John Lynde—whom, I would later learn from Lee Straight, was a master caster who gave lessons and exhibitions in the techniques outlined in his book as well as more spectacular demonstrations like casting two single-handed rods at once—set down clear precise directions on how to master Spey casting with one- and two-handed rods. One of the accompanying illustrative photos showed the author clutching a giant rod made of cane, or greenheart, to which was fastened a matching reel. This set up was a real heavy weight, yet Lynde appeared to be a slim fellow of average height. It was hard to imagine how he was able to wield such an outfit using anything resembling Faulkus' technique, which relied heavily upon power generated in the arms and shoulders. As I studied his book I realized that Lynde's teachings flowed from a need to make the manipulation of a heavy rod light work. In Lynde's style there is more reliance upon the entire body to support the motion of casting; the rod is anchored to it making it possible to minimize arm movements.

Fishing the Kispiox River. Darryl Hodgson's daughter Jill. Myron Kozak photo.

There were no extravagant claims in Lynde's work—unlike his modern counterparts he sought to instruct clearly and simply knowing that the entertainment was the end result of practice. With Lynde's help the double and single Spey casts came quickly. When a cast fell apart I recalled his lucid instruction, applied it by rote and stood amazed as the line rolled out over the water and placed my fly far out in the flow.

By late November I was ready. The weather had turned cold quickly. The Kalum was falling as quickly as the thermometer. I drove to the lower part of the river adjacent to the tree farm, since it is generally the most productive at that time of year, and tramped down the old skid trail through the first snowfall. Fresh tracks marked the unseen coming and goings of a moose, a rabbit and a wolf. At one point blood and the imprints of wings marked the kill of an eagle. The area had been logged some 30 years previously. Hardwoods, willow, dogwood and alder, are the forest now, to the benefit of the beavers, whose dam made crossing a deep side channel possible for me.

The pond was frozen as were the smaller ponds along the twisted trail. There were some small, dark objects in one. I stopped and knelt for a closer look. Juvenile salmon, scores of them, were suspended in the ice, trapped by the quick freeze. The reports had colder weather on the way. This would probably be my last opportunity to fish the river before the lower reaches turned into a skating rink. For that reason I hurried past The Eagle Tree, the inviting waters of the Upper Dump and Deep Creek to the most agreeable run for fly fishing, the Snake Run.

Ice rattled against the rocks protruding from the shallows. Farther out patches of the surface were glazed. Under the water white slush was attaching itself to the rocks. A spill in the river might prove fatal this far from the truck. I waded slowly with short steps thankful that, because of the long rod, there was no reason to wade past my knees. I made a short cast, then a longer one. The sinking tip I'd fastened to the double taper carried the hot pink prawn imitation I'd dubbed "Seafood" down far enough that I felt it bump against rocks as it swept through its arc. A few

casts later it stopped. A steady pulse was transmitted down the line as the first fish shook its head from side to side. After a short, dogged fight, I slid the fish through the slush to shore.

A small male with a hint of pink on its side, newly arrived, stood out brilliantly against the dark gray rocks. After extricating the hook, drying my hands then slipping them back into the woolen mitts, I started in again, and again a fish took hold, a larger animal, it turned out, a female, white and gray and shining with no hint of colour and translucent fins. So it went for the remainder of an afternoon when the Kalum would prove more generous than it had been before or has been since.

I'd never before—not even fishing warm summer water for aggressive summer steelhead—brought a score of steelhead to the fly. I thought about the situation as I made my way through the woods and across the frozen beaver ponds at dark. Clearly, I'd had the good fortune to intercept a fresh run of winter fish slowed down by the chill. I fired up the truck, listened to the diesel rattle and complain, drank black coffee, and waited for the cab to heat up. This, I thought, was as fine as steelheading gets: tranquillity, solitude, a hint of danger, and confirmation that a newly acquired strategy, learned after much diligent practice, would open new and exciting angling opportunities in the demanding, uncluttered surroundings of winter.

The Flies

The amount of fly fishing gear in the local tackle stores in Terrace is proof of the rapid growth of fly fishing in Skeena. When I first started fishing here there were only a few flies and a handful of fly tying materials to be had. Most of the flies sold in the local sports shops were gaudy, loosely assembled things whose best feature, according to their manufacturer, was the fact they were "hand tied". I wondered then, as I do now, how it could be otherwise: are some flies tied by dexterous craftsmen using their feet? Are fly tying automatons toiling away at their vises in dingy sweat shops turning out thousands of Royal Coachmen and Greenwell's' Glories?

Things have changed. In the local tackle emporiums you may now buy everything from dry flies small enough to float in a dew drop to articulated leeches the size of garden snakes, all of them, I'm told, tied by women in Thailand working for a company named after a river in Oregon. Despite the fact that these crafts mistresses have probably seen more tigers than they have trout their ability to ape, their digital dexterity, and their attention to detail have spawned some sturdy, beautifully built bugs.

Fly fishing curmudgeons like me insist on tying their own flies. We convince ourselves we are saving a wad of cash as we cart home little brown bag after little brown bag of expensive fly tying materials; we tell ourselves that our own inventions have some magic allure that "one of them store bought bugs", because it is tied by someone who has never slipped in a stream or caught an earlobe with an errant back cast, can't possibly possess.

Because the history of fly fishing in Skeena is short there are few native flies. I collect them, just as some people collect butterflies. For those of you who roll your own, following are the recipes.

Aston (Jim Aston)

Thread: Yellow.
Hook: Eagle Claw 1197 B or N, size 4.
Tail: Copper or silver Flashabou.
Body: Yellow tying thread.
Wing: Copper or silver Flashabou.

This is keeping things really simple. Jim Aston of Kitimat uses it for spring salmon. I have to grudgingly admit it works as well as any of my fancier Chinook patterns.

A Touch of Blue (Rob Brown)

Hook: Daiichi up eye salmon in a 2, 4 or 6.
Thread: Dark brown.
Tip: Seven turns of fine copper wire.
Tag: Dark blue Mylar tinsel.
Rib: Copper wire.
Body: Black wool yarn and black seal fur dubbed.
Hackle: Grizzly saddle dyed dark blue and a beard of hot orange schlappen.
Wing: Black bear.

Crepescule (Rob Brown)

Hook: The same as the previous fly.
Thread: Ditto.
Tag: Copper wire.
Tail: Pink hackle and golden pheasant dyed red.
Body: Plum purple wool yarn and purple seal.
Rib: Copper wire, fine.
Hackle: Purple with a beard of pink.
Wing: Dyed orange pheasant rump.

Tied by me for outings on rivers with dark bottoms and tea-coloured water.

Dynamite Stick (Anonymous)

Hook: Eagle Claw 1197 B or equivalent.
Thread: Red.
Tail: Magenta cock hackle.
Body: Magenta wool.
Rib: Gold oval tinsel.
Hackle: Magenta.
Wing: Red fox squirrel tail or brown bucktail.

I was given this pattern by an enthusiastic angler when I first began fishing Skeena steelhead. The young man proudly stated that his uncle, whose name I promptly forgot, invented the fly. I liked the name.

Esker Sculpin (Rob Brown)

Hook: Eagle Claw 1197 N.
Thread: Brown.
Body: None.
Wing: Gray squirrel tail and a few strands of pearl Mylar enclosed in two wide, dry-fly-quality grizzly hackles.
Throat: A tuft of hen hackle or polly yarn.
Head: Spun gray deer hair.

One spring day years ago, I dropped in on Dionys deLeeuw, who was then a managing biologist for the Fish and Wildlife Branch of the Ministry of Environment, Lands and Parks,

Region 6, and, to my surprise, found three Dolly Varden as long as his kitchen table is wide, lying there awaiting autopsy. Dionys had hooked the fish on salmon roe, but their stomachs showed that sculpins in gray and white camouflage were their meal of preference.

Dionys' big char came from Esker Bar. I hastily wrapped up this imitation and made my way there to catch some mammoth Dollies of my own, which I did—14 of them according to my diary, which also notes that the smallest was three pounds and the largest about three times as large as that. There is also an annotation about a 10-pound steelhead caught late in the windy afternoon of the same day.

Ferry Island Fancy (Laurie Parr)

Hook: Eagle Claw, size 6.
Tail: Blue Krystal Flash.
Body: Silver Mylar.
Wing: See tail.
Head: Pink chenille.

Ed Chapplow's recipe for sockeye. Since this pattern was popularized by him, the local tackle shops have difficulty keeping this invention of Laurie Parr's.

Float Chaser (Mike Whelpley)

Hook: Salmon light wire, in a 6 or 4.
Thread: Black.
Tail: A generous tuft of deer hair.
Body: Hot orange wool or glow yarn.
Hackle: Hot orange.
Wing: Deer hair.

Mike Whelpley created this hot version of Harry Lemire's Greased Liner and named it for those aggressive and perplexing winter steelhead that will ignore a gob of eggs and attempt to swallow a balsa wood float. With it he caught some late winter fish, no small achievement.

Green Butt Tube (Rob Brown)

Thread: Black.
Rib: Oval silver, medium.
Body: Black Phentex or black floss.
Butt: Fluorescent green wool.
Wing: A few strands of pearl Flashabou under polar bear hair.
Hook: A stick sharp bait hook in a size two. I like red plated ones, in keeping with the red tail of skunk patterns. Paradoxically, the small hooks hold better than the larger irons.

I tie this for Chinook. Using tubes enables you to construct a large but lightweight fly. The tubes can be purchased from British tackle manufacturers. Metal tubes can be purchased from the same firms but if you're in a hurry, model/hobby shops generally have a wide assortment of tubes made from different metals.

Lakelse Locomotive (Dan Gledhill)

Hook: Up eyed salmon, size 4.
Tail: Fibres from a gray owl.
Body: Pale yellow wool yarn.
Rib: Gold tinsel.
Hackle: Same as tail.
Wing: Raccoon fur.

I lost contact with Dan in the late seventies. Originally he moved north to ride shotgun on a group home, a job guaranteed to make mush of the human nervous system. In Dan's case taking care of those wayward adolescents sorely taxed his marriage.

After his marital relations blew apart, Dan was left with a stuffed owl, a raccoon pelt, his fishing rod, a multi-patched pair of Miner chest waders, and his welding tools. Using what he had on hand, he crafted what became his favourite steelhead pattern then took to the stream to salve his wounds.

You may substitute badger hackle or some other feather with a grayish cast; Dan won't mind.

Letham's Muddler (Phil Letham)

Hook: 2 to 2/0, an up eyed Mustad salmon hook. Phil's were Mustads.
Thread: 3/0 Black
Tail: A tuft of black marabou.
Body: Gold Mylar tubing.
Wings: Black marabou.
Collar: Spun gray deer hair, clipped at the bottom.
Head: Spun deer, occupying a third of the hook.

With its large head, this creature looks more like a rodent than a sculpin. Phil fished it almost exclusively on floating and sinking lines, with impressive results. The Mylar tubing is wound on like wool creating an almost indestructible body. The first marabou wing is set half way along the shank, the second is fastened on in the normal place. The deer hair is more a wing than a collar.

Mudflap (Rob Brown)

Hook: 3X long standard wire, heavily weighted.
Thread: Brown, standard diameter.
Body: Burlap.
Hackle: Pheasant rump.
Head: Deer hair clipped in the shape of a bullet.

This is what you get when you mix a Muddler, a Carey Special, and a Sack Fly. I'm responsible for the pattern. With it I've taken steelhead, coho, a few Chinook and many trout. I'd like to think the fish take it for a stonefly nymph, but I suspect they attack it because it offends their sensibilities.

This is an extravagant creation christened on the Dean, then later fished successfully on the Kispiox and Bulkley rivers. I wanted something with a Thunder and Lightning motif. The blue saddle is wound a la Art Lingren from the third turn of the rib. It gives the fly a compelling blue cast.

Olive Woolly Bugger (Public Domain)

Hook: 2X long, weighted.
Tail: Olive marabou.
Hackle: Palmered olive saddle.
Head: Olive chenille.

Some Belgian clients of Jim Culp's showed that this lake fly, when fished near the bottom, was irresistible to sockeye making their way up stream to Babine. A version with a muddled head does equally well.

Orange G.P. (Colonel Drury)

Thread: Hot orange.
Hook: 3/0 to 5/0.
Feelers: Polar bear hair dyed a dark fluorescent orange.
Eyes: One gold pheasant tippet feather dyed hot orange.

Body: Orange sparkle chenille.
Rib: Medium gold oval tinsel.
Legs: Wide hot orange cock hackle.
Carapace: Gold pheasant rump feathers dyed orange over dyed orange marabou.

B.C. angling veteran, Bob Taylor, introduced this pattern to B.C. streams. Art Lingren popularized a coal black version. I whipped this variation up for Chinook.

Partridge and Orange (Finlay Ferguson)

Hook: Standard wet fly, sizes 12 and 14.
Thread: Black.
Abdomen: Hot orange yarn or Swannundaze dressed thinly.
Thorax: A pinch of dark brown seal's fur.
Hackle: A few turns of brown or gray partridge.

Inspired by Sylvester Nemes' books on the soft hackled fly, Finlay decided that this adaptation would take steelhead. He was right. One memorable day, using a size 12, he took two fine summer-run Zymoetz steelhead that had resolutely ignored my larger, time-tested patterns. For cutthroat, Fin uses an olive bodied variation as well as the orange version, overwrapping them with clear vinyl as a defense against those toothy fish.

Polar Peril (Rob Brown)

Hook: Up eyed salmon. Sizes 4 and 6 (I use Japanese hooks for this pattern now).
Tail: Plum purple cock's hackle.
Body: Dark purple wool yarn.
Rib: Silver oval tinsel.
Hackle: See tail.
Wing: Polar bear.

A variation on the Purple Peril.

Polar and Red (Unknown)

Hook: Turned down eye. Eagle Claw or Mustad.
Thread: Black.
Tail: Red hackle.
Body: Red wool yarn.
Hackle: Red.
Wing: White polar bear hair.

According to the old-timers this was the only fly anyone used for quite some time. What is it about red that makes it so appealing to new anglers? Perhaps it grows from the school of angling theory that argues red makes fish angry. I think this is anthropomorphic. Yet, red still catches fish, even though almost nobody uses much material of that hue anymore.

Pynk Dynk (Doug Webb)

Hook: Size 4, 2X long.
Thread: Red.
Tail: Hot pink hackle.
Body: Hot pink wool yarn.
Hackle: Hot pink.
Wing: Bleached polar bear or white calf tail.

Doug Webb's colour blindness has led to some lurid patterns over the years. A typical snippet of streamside conversation between us might sound like this: "What do think of this orange

Aston

Jim Aston

A Touch of Blue

Rob Brown

Crepescule

Rob Brown

Dynamite Stick

Anonymous

Esker Sculpin

Rob Brown

Ferry Island Fancy

Laurie Parr

Float Chaser

Mike Whelpley

Green Butt Tube

Rob Brown

Lakelse Locomotive

Dan Gledhill

Letham's Muddler

Phil Letham

Mudflap

Rob Brown

Olive Woolly Bugger

Public Domain

Orange G.P.

Colonel Drury

Partridge and Orange

Finlay Ferguson

Polar Peril

Rob Brown

Polar and Red

Unknown

Pynk Dynk

Doug Webb

Riffle Cricket

Rob Brown

Seafood

Rob Brown

Shirley's Fancy

Roy Chapplow

Single Egg

Rob Brown

Skinny Skunk

Finlay Ferguson

Summer Muddler

Rob Brown

Trick or Treat

Doug Webb

Wintle's Wizard

Unclear

pattern I just tied up?" "Uh, Doug, that's green."

The colour of this one is unmistakable. For years Doug fished little else. Given the amount of roe in our rivers in late summer and early fall, and the dark complexion of many of our river bottoms, it's not surprising that flies with a pink hue do well.

Riffle Cricket (Rob Brown)

Hook: Light wire ring eyed.
Thread: Kevlar.
Tail: Black bear.
Body: Closed cell foam inside dubbed black hare fur.
Hackle: Grizzly or black, palmered.

Old sea dog, Pete Soverel, showed up here with some strange flies attached to his hat and vest. I bummed one from Pete and discovered they were simply unadorned bits of foam he'd lashed to a hook with some kind of navy knot. Even though Pete assured me these lures took fish, I had to dress them up into something resembling a fly. To this end I took his gift gave it a fur coat and spun a feather around it.

Naturally, I had to build some of my own foam bugs. Tying the foam on the hook proved difficult. After many less than happy experiments I came across a spool of wool, thin, gray wool yarn spun around a Kevlar core. If you secure the foam in three places, leaving two distinct humps in the process, the body won't turn and much of the floatation is preserved. Leaving a cowl of foam at the front of the fly is critical to the skating motion. As Pete promised, the fly floats like a battleship; it's the flagship in my armada of floating flies for summer steelhead.

Seafood (Rob Brown)

Hook: Eagle Claw 1197 nickel plate, sizes 2 and 4.
Thread: Hot orange.
Tail: Antennae, made from hot orange or pink latex.
Body: Orange sparkle chenille.
Hackle: A whole marabou plume in a pale pink.

This is one of my offspring. I tied it with cold, slow winter water in mind. I reasoned that soft supple material was required to give the impression of succulence. If steelhead mistake this for a prawn, which I strongly doubt, then it must be for a cooked one. The tails are tied long enough to wiggle.

Shirley's Fancy (Roy Chapplow)

Hook: Up eyed salmon style. A 4 is fine.
Thread: Black, regular strength.
Tail: Kingfisher blue cock hackle.
Body: Silver sparkle chenille.
Hackle: The same stuff as the tail.
Wing: Dark blue over green calf tail with a topping peacock sword.

Shirley Culp, smitten with the attractive materials that make up this dressing, asked Roy Chapplow, one of the few fly dressers in Terrace two decades ago, to make a fly from them. Shirley's Fancy was the result.

At that time the Culps ran a small tackle shop on Highway 16, two minutes away from the Copper River. Shirley's husband, Jim, decided the fly, despite its Yuletide aura, deserved a trial. For the field test Jim chose his favourite river, the Clore, the largest tributary of the Zymoetz. That day, late in

Skeena steelhead. Mike Whelpley photo.

November, a number of feisty little Clore fish chose Shirley's fancy fly over Pete Broomhall's darker patterns.

Single Egg (Rob Brown)

Hook: Wide gaped, short shanked variety, size 6.
Thread: Hot orange.
Body: A single plastic egg, small size over a body of flat silver Mylar.
Tail and Overbody: White Antron.

When is a fly not a fly? I'm willing to forego tradition and use this fly when eggs are rolling downstream. To make matters worse, I fish it on the end of a 12-foot leader and floating line affixing a small float made by threading a toothpick through a small green Corkie to the top of the leader. Originally I used an orange Corkie, but fish kept smacking it and disrupting the drift. When you use this set up in conjunction with a two-handed 14-foot rod, casting upstream and drifting back down drag free, you are actually float fishing. To dress the "fly" tie a very thin strand of white polypropylene wool so that it protrudes over the eye (the stuff I use is called Phentex, and can be obtained at K-Mart (during a blue light special if one is lucky), then wind on the flat Mylar. This done, debarb the hook then slide the egg over the shank as if you were impaling a worm. Now, bring the yarn rearward, atop the egg, lash it down and apply the cement. When the

Corkie twitches or hesitates, set the hook like a nymph fisher does.

Skinny Skunk (Finlay Ferguson)

Hook: Up eyed salmon, size 8. Heavy wire.
Thread: Black, 6/0.
Tail: A few fibres of red cock hackle. (dyed G.P. crest)
Rib: Fine silver tinsel.
Body: A thin strand of black wool yarn or tying thread.
Hackle: A few fibres of black hackle.
Wing: A few natural polar bear hairs.

It's nearly impossible to wrap this fly thin enough; Finlay's are anorexic. Since he fishes only a floating line year-round, Finlay wants his flies to penetrate the water column quickly. To facilitate this he uses a 10-foot level leader of 10-pound monofilament. In winter he'll employ the same pattern in a four or a two.

Summer Muddler (Rob Brown)

Hook: Tiemco TMC 200, sizes 6 and 4.
Thread: Brown.
Tail: Mottled Turkey, cocked upward.
Body: Gold Mylar (Diamond Braid is nice).
Wing: A pair of mottled turkey quills set over hot orange polar bear hair.
Hackle: A beard of dyed hot orange ring-necked pheasant rump fibres.
Collar: Dark brown deer hair spun 180 degrees on the top, creating a full wing thereby.
Head: Spun deer hair clipped.

Note: A lazy man's fly that fishes well on a floating line in the "greased line" method. Before the elegant TMC hooks I used 3X long Mustads. Its orange cast distinguishes this fly from so many similarly muddled dressings.

Trick or Treat (Doug Webb)

Hook: Up eyed salmon, size two.
Thread: Black or red.
Tail: Hot orange polar bear fur.
Body: Silver Mylar.
Hackle: Long black marabou plume.
Wing: Two strands of copper Flashabou tinsel under dyed hot orange polar bear fur.

Leech-like patterns are well known for their ability to sucker the steelhead of Skeena. Trout eat leeches, do steelhead? The adult Pacific lampreys are large, slippery creatures that can be seen scaling the rocky battlements of waterfalls with their lips (I'm not making this up) or spawning in the upper sections of rivers like the Morice or the Lakelse in spring.

Apparently these primitive fish are prolific. We discovered this when a research biologist, who soon became known as "the eel woman," hired Mike Whelpley to ferry her around the lower Skeena so that she could sniggle on the mud flats and sandbars there. Mike reported that eeling was something to behold: every time the woman zapped a clump of mud with her electroshocker, scores of lamprey larvae wiggled out of the mud.

In the juvenile stage of their existence, steelhead in this country must, from time to time, come in contact with the offspring of Pacific lamprey when the latter wiggle free from the mud like salmon fry squeezing out of the gravel, and make their way seaward. It's conceivable that the young steelhead gobble some of the slimy outmigrants, but whether the fish still carry an instinctual memory of such a meal when they return as adults, is a harder notion to entertain. More credible is the theory that the undulant motion of leech imitations provokes fish.

This eel of Webb's is as effective as the articulated or rabbit strip versions; in fact, I think it is more effective due to the radiant orange wing. Orange is always a good colour to build into a steelhead fly. Tie one and watch closely as it swings into the shallows. The copper tinsel flickers through the translucent wing. My theory is this sparkle reflects off the mirror helping fish to find it—of course this is typical angler science, unencumbered by scientific methodology, and should be regarded as more than a little suspect.

The marabou is wound on in the same manner one winds on a cock hackle. If obtaining polar bear fur is a problem—and really, none of us should use it—you may use one of the acrylic hair substitutes. Webb does, preferring to hang on to his waning supplies of polar hide.

Wintle's Wizard (Unclear)

Hook: Salmon style in 8, 6, or 4.
Tail: Dark mottled deer hair.
Body: Dubbed black seal fur.
Rib: Fine copper wire.
Hackle: A turn of grizzly.

There is some dispute about the origin of this simple and deadly fly. My investigations show it hatched somewhere near Oso, Washington. Bob Taylor, who made a lot of trips with Gerry Wintle to fish the Stilly in the days before the Deer Creek debacle, says the dressing is properly called The Spade Fly—a suitable name, for sure— and that Bob Arnold of Washington deserves paternity, yet in B.C. it carries Wintle's name. I asked Gerry about this. He raised his bushy eye brows and told me all he knew was that the fly was "born under the influence". Anyway, it showed up in lower Skeena on the end of Jim Culp's tippet. Our version opts for black seal, a material that is actually green and blue and black when you examine it closely. The copper rib is an attractive but unnecessary embellishment.

Last Word

The salvation for Skeena fisheries will ultimately lie in the adoption of selective systems of harvest in both fisheries and forestry. The giant corporations that have generated enormous profits denuding the temperate rain forests at the expense of the environment and, ultimately of local communities, are naturally loathe to give up their tenures in favour of wood lots and the slower pace of selective harvest. However, until community-based logging and the secondary manufacture of wood products is actively encouraged by BC's Ministry of Forests—until there is some

Des Nobles. Independent gillnetter, Prince Rupert, B.C. Myron Kozak photo.

47

Skeer

Skeena seine boat. Myron Kozak photo.

❦

loosening of the grip international forest giants have on the province's forests—the disastrous downstream effects of heavy-duty industrial forestry will continue to ravage our rivers. Steelhead, as others have correctly pointed out, are indicator species; their decreasing numbers measure the success of our environmental stewardship.

Over a century of commercial fishing at the mouth of the Skeena River, combined with interceptive fisheries further north, including the Alaska fisheries, and possibly the Asian high seas fishery, have taken a heavy toll on Skeena-bound salmon. As I write this there are encouraging signs that Federal fisheries managers are finally starting to act in accordance with a mandate that insists they put the health of the stocks before the requirements of users.

The Skeena Watershed Committee is a body consisting of natives, sportsmen, commercial fishermen, and representatives of the fishing industry, who are provided with information by bureaucrats and scientists from the federal and provincial government agencies charged with overseeing the fisheries. As a result of the deliberations of this democratically representative committee an annual fishing plan is brought forward. In its maiden year of operation the committee ratified a plan that reduced considerably the kill of steelhead and summer coho. Moreover, the committee showed a distinct inclination toward selective harvesting methods. I know of no other fishery in the world where such disparate groups get together and struggle for consensus. There is hope here.

Gene Llewellyn and Finlay Ferguson have felt the pulse of the rivers feeding the lower Skeena; they have experienced some of the best fishing it has to offer. Sadly, they agree that steelheading here is fragile and failing. The quality of angling is poorer. Though they fervently hope it will be otherwise, they concede that the golden age for the steelhead of the lower Skeena might have passed.

Still, there remain exciting rivers to explore and unknown runs waiting to be discovered. Getting to them is difficult and expensive, but the opportunity to catch a fish in uncharted territory is the best, most fulfilling experience angling has to offer. It balances diminished and lost opportunities.

❦

Lower Skeena after the storm. Mike Whelpley photo.